Mindfulness
at Work
In A Week

Clara Seeger is a neuroleadership coach, corporate facilitator, speaker and author, specializing in mindfulness and emotional intelligence. Oxford-educated (MA, M.Phil.) and with a Ph.D. in German literature, she worked in investment banking before training as a coach. Clara works with international companies across many sectors and countries, delivering mindfulness interventions, leadership development courses and coach training.

Following her completion of an M.Sc. in 'Mindfulness: Neuroscience and clinical applications' (Distinction) at King's College London, Clara developed her own mindfulness-based coaching methodology and is passionate about introducing the benefits and neuroscience of mindfulness to the corporate world, both theoretically and practically. She has written several articles on neuroleadership and banking as well as *Investing in Meaning: An alternative approach to leveraging your portfolio* (Completely Novel, 2012), a coaching book for helping professionals maximize their sense of meaning at work.

For my parents and my brother, my husband, Marco, and my children, Alexis and Philippos, for all their love and encouragement.

Mindfulness at Work In A Week

Clara Seeger

Teach Yourself®

First published in Great Britain in 2016 by John Murray Learning. An Hachette UK company.

Copyright © Clara Seeger 2016

The right of Clara Seeger to be identified as the Author of the Work has been asserted by her in accordance with the Copyright, Designs and Patents Act 1988.

Database right Hodder & Stoughton (makers)

The *Teach Yourself* name is a registered trademark of Hachette UK.

British Library Cataloguing in Publication Data: a catalogue record for this title is available from the British Library.

Library of Congress Catalog Card Number: on file.

Paperback ISBN 978 1 473 60764 4

Ebook ISBN 978 1 473 60765 1

2

The publisher has used its best endeavours to ensure that any website addresses referred to in this book are correct and active at the time of going to press. However, the publisher and the author have no responsibility for the websites and can make no guarantee that a site will remain live or that the content will remain relevant, decent or appropriate.

The publisher has made every effort to mark as such all words which it believes to be trademarks. The publisher should also like to make it clear that the presence of a word in the book, whether marked or unmarked, in no way affects its legal status as a trademark.

Every reasonable effort has been made by the publisher to trace the copyright holders of material in this book. Any errors or omissions should be notified in writing to the publisher, who will endeavour to rectify the situation for any reprints and future editions.

Typeset by Cenveo® Publisher Services.

Printed and bound in Great Britain by CPI Group (UK) Ltd., Croydon, CR0 4YY.

John Murray Learning policy is to use papers that are natural, renewable and recyclable products and made from wood grown in sustainable forests. The logging and manufacturing processes are expected to conform to the environmental regulations of the country of origin.

John Murray Learning
Carmelite House
50 Victoria Embankment
London EC4Y 0DZ
www.hodder.co.uk

Also available in ebook

Contents

Introduction

There is an increasing awareness of, and appetite for, mindfulness across the corporate world, mostly mediated through mindfulness-trained coaches and leadership facilitators, as well as an increasing body of neuroscientific research, which has underpinned this ancient contemplative practice with solid scientific inquiry and proof of its innumerable benefits. With chronic stress taking its toll, leading to burnout and impaired decision-making, many employees and corporate executives have realized that a new approach to working life is needed. Mindfulness is a tool that helps calm the mind through the conscious and intentional directing of one's attention. It can enhance focus, reduce stress, improve performance, facilitate decision-making, increase self-control and raise your level of wellbeing.

In the UK, for example, the importance of mindfulness to society at large has now officially been recognized by the Mindfulness All-Party Parliamentary Group, which in 2015 published a report containing a number of recommendations for implementing mindfulness in both the private and public sector to combat stress and improve organizational effectiveness. It also encourages the commissioning of scientific research into the effectiveness of mindfulness as an occupational health intervention in addressing issues such as stress, work-related rumination, fatigue and disrupted sleep.

As a growing number of organizations and their staff are espousing mindfulness to deal with stress and increase productivity, I am increasingly being invited to lead workshops on mindfulness by my corporate clients from an array of different sectors.

If you, like many of my clients, work for a large company and are faced with the multiple challenges and demands of corporate life – working to tight deadlines, multi-tasking, decision-making under pressure, technology overwhelm, managing a team, office politics, 24/7 availability, job insecurity and market volatility – then *Mindfulness at Work* is written for you.

In addition to the countless technical skills and expertise needed, such demanding work requires high levels of emotional intelligence, personal effectiveness, skilful communication, a clear head, good judgement, planning and organizational skills, self-control, insightfulness, creativity, energy and focus. I would argue – and can call upon a growing body of scientific research to back this up – that mindfulness can help with all of these skills. In fact, it may well be the single most useful and beneficial practice you could adopt in both your life and your work.

Mindfulness is a quality of our consciousness, a particular relationship to our experience that anybody can adopt at any time while going about one's daily life. This makes it an ideal practice for busy employees and managers.

Mindfulness does not need to be studied theoretically for it to work. It does need to be *practised*, however. Even a few minutes of regular practice are beneficial and can easily be integrated into your work.

Mindfulness at Work explains in simple and practical terms what mindfulness is, the brain science behind it, and how it can positively impact on many crucial areas of work life. You will learn tips and techniques on how to integrate mindful awareness into your daily work to improve wellbeing, thinking and performance.

Clara Seeger

SUNDAY

What is mindfulness?

Before we delve into the different aspects of working life to explore how they can be enhanced through mindfulness we need to understand what mindfulness really is. We will introduce you to the best-known definition of mindfulness by the 'father' of mindfulness in the West, Jon Kabat-Zinn, and unpack it to reveal its three central tenets. Further, we will learn about different types of mindfulness practices, both formal and informal, as well as their purpose, and identify their wide-ranging benefits that have been established through scientific studies in different contexts, not just clinical research but also work that has been conducted in the workplace.

Next, we will look at the mechanisms through which mindfulness exerts its effects and review the main changes in brain structure and function that have been established through scientific studies so far.

To conclude, you will be introduced to a basic breath meditation as well as some tips for informal practices that you can start integrating into your day as you set off on your path towards increased mindfulness, greater wellbeing and inner peace.

A definition

So what do we mean by the term 'mindfulness', which has become so ubiquitous these days, yet remains somewhat elusive and more multi-dimensional than most definitions suggest? The most widely used definition stems from Jon Kabat-Zinn who is to be credited for making this ancient Buddhist practice widely accessible to mainstream society.

Having adapted mindfulness from its spiritual roots to the needs of chronic-pain patients in the form of a structured eight-week Mindfulness-Based Stress Reduction (MBSR) programme back in the late 1970s, Kabat-Zinn describes the practice as a form of 'paying attention in a particular way: on purpose, in the present moment, and non-judgementally' (Kabat-Zinn 1994). Unpacking this definition, three key elements of mindfulness can be identified:

1 Mindfulness is something you do **intentionally** rather than by accident.
2 Mindfulness is about paying **attention** in the **present** moment.
3 Mindfulness requires a certain **attitude** towards what you are doing.

These three central axioms of mindfulness have been captured diagrammatically in the following conceptual model by Shapiro et al. (2006):

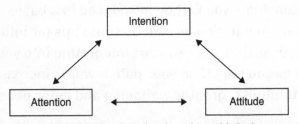

The three axioms of mindfulness – Intention, Attention and Attitude – are not separate stages. They are interwoven aspects of a single cyclic process and occur simultaneously. Mindfulness is this moment-to-moment process.

Let's look at these three elements in more detail.

Intention

Paying attention does not simply occur; it is a purposeful activity, driven by the powerful intention to inhabit the realm of awareness and to be fully present for one's experience, whatever this may be. Before each 'formal' practice it is important to set an intention, which is different from a goal: it is not about reaching a certain outcome (in fact, you are explicitly urged to let go of any such attachments to outcomes!) but about committing oneself to practising in a certain way; this could be anything from focusing on the breath, to being open to whatever may arise, to being kind to oneself for losing focus for the umpteenth time (because you will!). Intentions drive the practice and give it purpose, coherence and meaning.

Attention

In terms of attention, this is widely considered to be the central component of mindfulness, which is often, somewhat reductively, seen as nothing more than attention training. It is undoubtedly a crucial aspect of mindfulness and one that is trained in all forms of mindfulness exercise, particularly when practising breath meditation. It involves directing one's focus and sustaining it on the desired object of attention (usually the breath), while renouncing other stimuli.

The important part about paying attention is that it necessarily occurs in the present moment. This may sound banal, but how often do you really practise this? Our mind tends to wander, casting itself back to some episode in the past that is still lingering and usurping mental space, or is consumed by plans and to do lists that take us far away into the future. Being present for all of our experience, which, after all, only ever unfolds in the present moment, is the greatest gift that we can learn to give ourselves through practising mindfulness. Present-moment awareness is very simple in principle, but, in practice, it goes against many years of hardwired mental habits of 'time travelling', as it has facetiously been called in the literature. Paying attention in the present moment entails noticing what is going on both within us, our thoughts, feelings and physical sensations, as well as in the outside world.

Attitude

When you notice what is going on inside and around you, it is important to do so non-judgementally, without criticizing yourself for whatever arises in your mind or wishing things to be different. It is entirely normal to experience difficulties when trying to pay attention in the moment as the mind's natural state is to wander and engage in daydreaming, fantasizing, reminiscing, planning and so on, and to switch seamlessly and often erratically from one mental excursion to another, something that the Buddhists call 'monkey mind'. As one has set an intention to sustain the focus on the breath or any other object of attention in the present moment, it is easy to get frustrated and engage in self-critical and judgemental thinking, condemning oneself for failing to follow the instructions to the letter. Yet, unlike any other new practice that you may decide to take up, an accepting attitude is part of the very instructions and an essential ingredient in what you are asked to follow. And this is how mindfulness practice is very different from any other skill you may have learned: rather than aiming at perfect execution, it is content with remaining a 'practice', insisting on you making your peace with imperfection and doing so with a kind and self-compassionate attitude.

What you do

Broadly speaking, mindfulness can be practised in two mutually enhancing ways: first, by way of **formal practices** where you sit, stand, lie or walk mindfully for a predetermined length of time and follow the instructions from your teacher, a tape or even your own, and second, **informally**, by integrating mindfulness into your everyday life and activities, doing what you do anyway, but doing so in a non-habitual, mindful fashion.

Formal practices

The two most common formal practices are breath meditation where the breath is used as the anchor and object of attention (**shamata**), aimed at steadying the mind, practising narrow-focus concentration and calming the nervous system, and the more advanced insight meditation (**vipassana**), which aims at eliciting deeper insights into the nature of impermanence and the interconnectness of all phenomena and thus at attaining wisdom. Shamata is considered a prerequisite for wisdom and insight – only a steady mind can achieve enlightenment. The most common posture is sitting, either on a cushion on the floor or on a straight-back chair, the spine erect but not stiff, the eyes closed or cast downwards, the posture signalling alertness and dignity, rather than pure relaxation. In shamata meditation, the breath is used as a tool to steady the mind and to ground it in present-moment awareness. The breath has the advantage of being easily available to us at all times and being intimately connected to the present: you can only ever breathe in the present moment, which makes the breath ideally suited as an object of mindfulness meditation.

Observing your breath means following it for the duration of each in-breath, as well as each out-breath, without wanting to change it in any way or making it different from what it is. You can focus on the sensations of the air on your upper lip as it moves in and out of your nostrils or feel your abdomen rising with each in-breath and falling with each out-breath, wherever you feel it most strongly. When you notice your mind wandering away from the breath, as it inevitably will, gently but firmly bring it back to the breath, remembering to maintain a non-judgemental attitude towards yourself. Learn to treat the realization that the mind has wandered as an achievement, rather than a failure, a sign that you have woken up and become aware.

In addition to this basic sitting meditation you can practise a so-called 'body scan' meditation lying down, where you shine the spotlight of attention on each part of the body in turn, gradually working up from your feet to the top of your head. Furthermore, you can practise mindful movement where you engage in gentle stretches or subtle yoga movements, exploring your physical edge in a non-competitive and accepting manner. Finally, mindful walking is a practice that brings present-moment awareness into each and every aspect of walking and thus constitutes a transitional practice between formal and informal practices.

Informal practices

By informal practices we mean practices that bring mindfulness into your everyday life, for example making your tea mindfully or taking a mindful shower, brushing your teeth or doing the dishes mindfully. The idea here is to transfer what you have learned from the formal practices and integrating this firmly into your daily life, making you fully aware of all aspects of your experience in the present moment and thus creating a richer and more consciously experienced reality than normally tends to be the case. We rarely register seemingly banal details such as the sensation of the toothbrush's bristles against our gums, and, by extension, we may overlook more significant moments, a smile, a kind word, the sound of our children's laughter or the warmth of the sun on our skin. We are so used to mentally fast-forwarding our life to the next important milestone that we often miss the richness of our everyday moments in the process. Yet these moments are all we ever have as the past and future only exist in our imagination and are ultimately insubstantial. As Kabat-Zinn reminds us, we have only moments to live. In other words, if these moments right here, right now, are all we ever have, they are precious – we might as well turn up and live them to the full!

Benefits

The impact of mindfulness practice on a wide variety of different aspects of human functioning has been firmly established in an enormous body of academic studies, which is growing exponentially. The list of salutary effects on our

physical, mental and intellectual wellbeing is seemingly
endless, impacting on virtually every aspect of life:

Physical	Emotional	Intellectual/mental
Lower blood pressure	Better emotional regulation	More mental clarity
Stronger immune system	More calm	Better focus and concentration
Slower ageing (telomere lengthening)	More wellbeing/ happiness	Better memory
Improved cardiovascular health	Enhanced emotional intelligence	Increased attention span
Quicker recovery time from surgery, illnesses	Less reactivity	Improved decision-making
Faster healing of wounds	Increased resilience	Better problem-solving
Less inflammation	More self-compassion	Enhanced cognitive flexibility
Lower stress levels	Reduced depressive relapse	Less rumination
	Less emotional volatility	More creativity
	Less anxiety	Less mental proliferation
		More self-awareness

Workplace benefits

It is easy to see how this ever-growing list of beneficial effects
can also be of great service in the workplace, and a number of
specific workplace benefits have already been identified in the
academic literature:

- better focus and concentration
- lower stress levels
- better self-control and emotional regulation
- higher empathy and emotional intelligence
- improved relationships
- better decision-making

- improved job satisfaction and engagement
- lower absenteeism due to sickness
- improved creativity and innovation
- enhanced productivity and performance.

The evidence is so strong that a number of mindfulness-based interventions and training courses have been created or adapted for workplace requirements and numerous books have been written on the subject of mindfulness in the workplace. As mindfulness is becoming increasingly mainstream, a growing number of CEOs and high-profile business figures are 'coming' out as being long-term meditators, many of whom we will encounter in the course of this book.

> *'When I went on holiday with my family recently, I wasn't afraid to switch on my out-of-office email message. When was the last time you did the same? If you can't recall, then maybe it's time to slow down, switch off your phone and focus on the present. Your business will benefit as a result.'*
>
> Richard Branson, Founder of Virgin

Mindfulness shapes our brain

So how does mindfulness produce such countless beneficial effects on human functioning? The last 20 years have seen immense advances in the field of neuroscience, and mindfulness has attracted considerable interest from scientists, keen to explain its mechanisms of change. The discovery of neuroplasticity, the capacity of the brain to rewire itself and produce new neurons even in adults (neurogenesis), has opened our eyes to the fact that the specific content of our consciousness (external stimuli plus our thoughts, emotions and body sensations) as well as the quality of attention that we bestow on it, can all exert a lasting influence on our brain.

What and how we think literally changes our brain! Mental connections are strengthened and embedded through repeated or prolonged use, while others that are no longer needed will eventually atrophy. Through mindfulness we can thus change the way our brain is wired – for the better. In the famous words of the neuroscientist Donald Hebb, 'neurons that fire together, wire together.' But before we explore how mindfulness changes and shapes our brain, let us have a brief look at what it is precisely about mindfulness that effects these changes.

A review by neuroscientist Britta Hoelzel and colleagues (2011) has identified four key mechanisms acting on the brain – attention regulation, body awareness, emotion regulation and a change in perspective on the self – all of which interact closely to bring about an entire range of the benefits, as outlined above.

1 Attention regulation

The first mechanism can be split into attention on internal states and attention on external states. Meditators who are trained in focused attention (i.e. attention on a single object such as the breath, sounds, etc.) have an improved capacity to concentrate on a single task for longer, enabling them to renounce distraction and reduce ineffective multitasking.

2 Body awareness

Body awareness describes the ability to notice subtle physical sensations. Attention to internal states increases interoception, the ability to attend to and be perceptive of sensory and emotional information and cues from within, creating greater self-awareness and as a corollary, self-management – two of the cornerstones of emotional intelligence. The ability to notice your emotional and physical state without reacting to it in the usual automatic and often dysfunctional way enables you to regulate such states, which is especially important if they are somewhat unpleasant or difficult. You learn just to 'sit with them', let them be, focusing your attention on their specificity rather than on how to avoid them, fight them or fix them. This non-reactivity in itself is healing and can be very liberating – freeing yourself from the perennial tendency to solve problems, overcome obstacles and strive for achievements, which has been defined as the 'doing mode'. Whatever the situation is and however you may find it, if it is already there, it would be unwise to spend any energy on feeding a state of inner resistance or resentment to it. If there is any skilful action to be taken to alleviate or change such a state, you are more likely to identify what needs to be done if you first accept the reality of what is happening as it is happening, in all its dimensions. Such increased alertness can thus contribute to more conscious and wiser decision-making.

It has been argued that internal awareness of one's own experience is a prerequisite for empathy. The brain regions associated in interoception (most notably the insula and the temporo-parietal junction) are also implicated in social cognition and empathic responses. It is through this mechanism that mindfulness can thus improve social awareness and relationship management, the other two building blocks of emotional intelligence, as measured by the Emotional Competence Inventory, published by The Hay Group.

3 Emotion regulation

By emotion regulation we mean the modification of emotional responses through the intervention of regulatory processes. Evidence suggests that even mindfulness novices show a reduction in emotional interference (the delay in reaction time after being shown emotive pictures, which indicates less emotional reactivity) after just seven weeks of training. Physiological studies have also found decreased emotional reactivity as measured by reduced skin conductance in response to negative stimuli, as well as a quicker recovery time from emotional upsets. We will explore the topic of emotion regulation in more depth on Thursday.

4 Change in perspective on the self

One of the key mechanisms of mindfulness is its promotion of metacognitive awareness and insight: when you practise mindfulness you are not only paying attention or being mindful but you *know* that you are being mindful. As you are observing your thoughts, emotions and body sensations you are not only aware of these as specific *contents* of your consciousness but aware of yourself as the consciousness in which these phenomena can arise. Mindfulness is thus a *quality* of consciousness rather than being tied to specific contents of mind – these only serve as the training ground through which the mind becomes aware of itself.

The practice of mindfulness is thus not only the act of paying attention itself but the awareness of this act. When you are mindful you are no longer the protagonist in your personal drama but the omniscient observer who watches the drama unfold, can see the big picture as well as the details, and can remain disinterested and dispassionate, not carried away in the ebb and flow of ever-changing experiences. This dis-identification from the contents of your consciousness, based on the observation of their constant state of flux, ultimately leads to the dissolution of the sense of self in the narrow sense of a stable, unchanging, separate entity.

The mechanism of metacognitive awareness has far-reaching benefits, most notably in the clinical context where it has been identified as the key mindfulness element in the prevention of recurrent depressive relapse, and has made it into the UK's National Institute for Health and Care Excellence (NICE) guidelines as mindfulness-based cognitive therapy (MBCT). In this, an adaptation of MBSR for depression, people with three or more previous depressive episodes learn to nip the onset of ruminative thinking in the bud by recognizing their negative thoughts as merely 'mental events' of no real substance. This process of 'decentring' or 'reperceiving' is a useful skill even beyond the condition of depression and can foster emotion regulation, clarity of mind and inner peace.

Brain changes

Based on the four components outlined above, neuroimaging studies have established that mindfulness promotes neuroplasticity in areas of the brain that are repeatedly engaged during formal practice. Here is an overview of the major scientific findings, testifying to the structural and functional brain changes detected in experienced meditators:

- Meditators have greater cortical thickness (i.e. more cortical tissue on the outer shell of the brain) compared to non-meditators in areas associated with
  - **sustained attention and cognition-emotion integration** (right prefrontal cortex, Brodmann Areas 9/10). In 40- to 50-year-old meditators, the cortical thickness of this area was found to be comparable to that of 20 - to 30-year-old meditators and controls, suggesting that regular meditation practice may slow down the rate of neural degeneration in prefrontal areas where it is most pronounced.
  - **interoception**, the awareness of internal body states (right anterior insula)
  - **sensory processing** (somatosensory cortex)
  - the **connection between self and others** (right inferior occipito-temporal cortex). This area has been shown to correlate most strongly with the amount of meditation experience of practitioners.
- Meditators have significantly higher grey matter concentration and volume in the **hippocampus** (a region important for learning and memory processes which also puts things in perspective by down-regulating the alarm bell in the brain, the amygdala), particularly in a sub-region involved in stress regulation.

In terms of functional changes, the following effects have been identified in long-term meditators by the use of functional magnetic resonance imaging (fMRI):

- reduced activation in the default mode network, which is involved in mind wandering and self-referential thinking

- less mental fixation and elaboration, evident in faster disengagement of brain areas during semantic processing, suggesting that meditators are better able to control the automatic proliferation of thinking
- more openness to negative experience (e.g. pain), demonstrated by activation of the pain network (thalamus, insula, amygdala) but deactivation of areas involved in pain reactivity and distress (prefrontal and anterior cingulate cortex)
- Increased activation on the left side of the prefrontal cortex, which is associated with positive emotion, better mood and creativity.

Mindfulness on the job

One of the reasons people are sometimes reluctant to take up a regular mindfulness practice is because they are pressed for time. We all are. It is a sign of our times not to have time to spare. The good news about mindfulness practice is that it does not necessarily require much time. Beneficial as it is to have a daily sitting practice of 20 minutes, this is not always practical in periods of high pressure, when you are working to tight deadlines, are on a business trip or have to work incredibly long hours as well as having a family to look after when you get home.

However, the good news is that mindfulness is a quality of mind, a lifestyle choice, if you will, to live your life fully and consciously. You do not necessarily need to take time out or practise in a dedicated area (although having a regular space for your formal practice can indeed be helpful). Mindfulness needs to be practised in daily life, not just on the cushion or the chair. You can practise on the job, as it were. In fact, the real litmus test for the effectiveness of your mindfulness practice is to be able to integrate it into your life.

Here are some tips on daily opportunities for mindful awareness of the breath that can easily slot into your daily work without the need to sit cross-legged on the office floor.

Mindful breathing

Throughout the working day, return to your breathing, becoming aware that you are breathing, without changing it in any way. Notice when your breathing is deep and slow and when it speeds up or becomes shallow. As the Zen Buddhist teacher Thich Nhat Hanh suggests, it may help to say to yourself the following words while you are following your breath:

'Breathing in, I am aware of my in-breath. Breathing out, I am aware of my out-breath. Breathing in, I am aware of my body. Breathing out, I release the tension in my body.'

You can do this at any time, for example in the following situations:

- as you travel to work by car, train or bus
- as you enter your office and walk up to your desk
- as you greet or engage with colleagues
- as you wait for the kettle to boil or the water to fill your glass
- as you walk to the bathroom
- as you eat your lunch
- as you have a drink
- as you sit and work at your computer
- on your journey home.

'Just watch this moment, without trying to change it at all. What is happening? What do you feel? What do you see? What do you hear?'

Jon Kabat-Zinn, Professor of Medicine Emeritus and creator of the Stress Reduction Clinic and the Center for Mindfulness in Medicine, University of Massachusetts Medical School

Summary

Today we learned what mindfulness is: a form of present-moment awareness, practised intentionally and with an open and non-judgemental attitude. We looked at the history of how this ancient practice was introduced to Western culture through the work of Jon Kabat-Zinn and distinguished between formal practices to help you build your 'mindfulness muscle' and informal practices to apply and integrate this quality of consciousness into your daily life. Further, we identified some of the manifold physical, emotional and mental benefits that have been established through scientific experiments, as well as their impact on the workplace.

We then outlined the four mechanisms through which mindfulness exerts its beneficial influence. We also learned how mindfulness practice can change both the structure and function of the brain in beneficial ways, leading to larger volume in areas associated with attention, learning and memory, interoception and a smaller fear centre, as well as more activation on the left side of the prefrontal cortex,

SUNDAY
MONDAY
TUESDAY
WEDNESDAY
THURSDAY
FRIDAY
SATURDAY

associated with positive emotions and creativity. Finally, we shared a simple breath meditation and some tips on where and when mindfulness can be practised on the job.

Fact-check (answers at the back)

1. Which of the following elements is *not* part of the definition of mindfulness?
   a) Relaxation ❑
   b) Intention ❑
   c) Attitude ❑
   d) Present-moment awareness ❑

2. Mindful attention entails a focus on
   a) The past ❑
   b) The future ❑
   c) The present moment ❑
   d) Time travelling ❑

3. Your meditation posture should embody
   a) Relaxation ❑
   b) Alertness ❑
   c) Fun ❑
   d) Happiness ❑

4. What is the purpose of informal practices?
   a) To entertain you in everyday life ❑
   b) To practise meditation in a more relaxed way ❑
   c) To get better at your daily tasks ❑
   d) To live consciously ❑

5. Neuroplasticity denotes
   a) The brain's plastic-like texture ❑
   b) The brain's ability to change and rewire itself ❑
   c) The neurons' similarity to Plasticine ❑
   d) Brain surgery ❑

6. Which benefits does attention training yield?
   a) A longer attention span ❑
   b) More multitasking ❑
   c) Fewer distractions ❑
   d) More interesting work ❑

7. What does a reduction of emotional interference suggest about mindfulness?
   a) It helps you experience fewer upsetting emotions ❑
   b) It makes you no longer care about your experience ❑
   c) It helps you regulate your emotions better ❑
   d) Emotions will not interfere with your daily life ❑

8. What is meant by metacognitive awareness?
   a) Awareness of all phenomena ❑
   b) Awareness of internal states ❑
   c) Awareness of our cognitions ❑
   d) Awareness of our self ❑

9. How can metacognitive awareness help with depression?
   a) It leads to less negative thinking ❑
   b) It lifts your mood ❑
   c) It helps you focus on something else ❑
   d) It helps you 'decentre' from your thoughts and feelings ❑

10. Which change in brain structure or function has *not* been identified as a result of mindfulness practice?
    a) A larger amygdala ❑
    b) A larger hippocampus ❑
    d) More activation of the left frontal area ❑
    d) A stronger insula ❑

MONDAY

Paying attention mindfully

Attention may not be a topic one expects to find in a book teaching workplace skills, yet attention is absolutely fundamental to so many different aspects of working life that it deserves pride of place in this book: it is essential to learning, storage and retrieval of information, professional effectiveness, cognitive flexibility and adaptability, decision-making and cultivating a positive mental attitude.

Nevertheless, the modern workplace makes impossible demands on our attention: working in an open-plan office is the norm, multitasking is an unwritten expectation in most job descriptions, as is juggling the constant stream of emails, phone calls, around-the-clock availability, endless meetings and relentless business trips as part of the working week. Today's employees are expected to possess inexhaustible attentional resources and to switch the focus of their attention between processes and interactions at the drop of a hat.

As we will see below, both expectations are entirely unrealistic and many corporate employees suffer from what has been termed **attention deficit trait** (ADT) due to too much input and a hyperkinetic working environment. Today we will explore what attention is, why it is so crucial to develop, why it can be tricky to achieve and how mindfulness might help us train this muscle.

What is attention and why is it crucial in the workplace?

We live in the information age brought about by the digital revolution. Our economy is based on information computerization and a large proportion of our modern workforce is employed by the information industry. Even in our free time, information is ubiquitous, freely available and often overwhelming. The difficulty is no longer the availability or even reliability of the information but the filtering out of what is appropriate and relevant, while ensuring that we do not miss potentially vital information.

Information processing and information overload

This is where attention comes in: it is a crucial part of information processing. It helps us select relevant and discard irrelevant information. There are numerous different and at times contradictory theories of attention but most of them agree on the premise that attention is **selective** and in **limited supply** due to our finite pool of attentional resources. Many early researchers have proposed so-called 'bottleneck' theories of attention, which are centred around the notion that the processing of information is conducted via a single channel, meaning that we can only process information sequentially rather than simultaneously (Pashler & Johnston 1998). Later theorists stress the idea of attention as a 'selective distribution of a limited amount of cognitive resources' (Smith & Kosslyn 2013) in a dynamic process by which the selection of information for further processing goes hand in hand with the inhibition of other information.

Top-down versus bottom-up processing

Out of the countless items of incoming stimuli our brain only ever selects a small fraction of information for further processing. This selection process is driven both from the '**top down**' by our goals at any one time (not just the bigger goals in our life but also small, daily objectives such as searching for a particular news item on the Internet or browsing through a set of charts to find the most relevant one to include in your report) and from the '**bottom up**' by salient sensory stimuli in our environment (e.g. a sudden fire alarm or the sound of breaking glass that automatically grabs our attention). Neuroscientists have discovered that two distinct neural networks are at play when we engage our attention in a goal-oriented versus a stimulus-driven fashion. While top-down attentional networks involve frontal and dorsal parietal areas, stimulus-driven attentional networks engage a more ventral system (Corbetta & Shulman 2002). The two networks are functionally independent but interactive.

This combination of goal- and stimulus-driven information processing enables us to function and make decisions from day to day, to achieve our goals while safeguarding our wellbeing, and to deal with the uncertainty that would otherwise paralyse us.

Having said this, useful and necessary as it is, the selectivity of our perception may also lead to problems and even distress as we inevitably distort and misconstrue sometimes vital signs or clues, leading to misconceptions and a more or less unconscious bias in our decision-making. This can have potentially dangerous consequences in the corporate world.

Corporate challenges on our attention

The limitations of our attentional capacity in combination with individual differences in our ability to pay attention pose several challenges within a corporate context, which all pertain to our capacity for attentional control – the deliberate directing of attention to the specific task at hand or the rapid shifting of attention from one task to another. The normal, innate challenges to our attention are often exacerbated in a corporate environment due to the specific external, non-conducive conditions outlined above and can be summarized as follows:

- remaining focused on the job at hand for a prolonged time (e.g. finishing a report or presentation, conducting a meeting, creating a spreadsheet)
- managing external distractions (e.g. phone calls, unscheduled conversations, meetings, emails, office noise)
- disengaging from the source of external distractions back to the task at hand
- managing our internal appetite for stimulation (e.g. the urge to be part of a conversation, surfing the web, looking for a new task/challenge)
- switching of attention from one task to another, driven by external demands beyond one's control.

The cost of divided attention

These common attentional challenges may all lead to a potentially perilous impairment of the quality of our attention – divided attention – that impacts on our effectiveness and efficiency in the daily handling of our job responsibilities but which, in the worst-case scenario, can also have serious consequences for decision-making. Divided attention severely compromises not only the speed at which we accomplish our tasks (Shapiro et al. 1994) but also, most importantly, their quality (Neisser & Becklen 1975). Our brain is simply not designed to do more than one thing at a time without paying a price. In cognitive neuroscience this impairment caused by the simultaneous handling of two tasks is labelled 'dual-task interference'. Translated into the business context, this price is called 'performance' and no employee or business can afford to pay it in the long term.

Moreover, in business we are usually not just faced with interference from dual tasks but from (the clearly misguided expectation of) multitasking. One obvious area where performance will suffer from divided attention is learning and memory, as the brain will encounter problems encoding and subsequently retrieving information that has not been properly attended to. The problem is, however, that employees as well as organizations often only become aware of this compromise in the quality of attention when there is a serious problem.

Given our brain's capacity to change as a result of paying focused attention, it is thus extremely important to be conscious of, and intentional about, what we pay attention to. Both good and bad habits are a product of the attention economy in the brain. By focusing on the 'right' object and in the 'right' way (i.e. with awareness) we can influence how our brain may change in response to our attentional habits.

Key learning points about attention

- Attention shapes the brain (neuroplasticity) – what you attend to will become hardwired.
- Attention is limited and selective.
- Attention can occur from the top down (goal-driven) and from the bottom up (stimulus-driven).
- Focused (i.e. undivided) attention is needed for sustainable learning and memory – you can retain only what you attended to.
- Focused attention is needed for performance accuracy and speed – focus on one task at a time to ensure top performance.

TIP *Divided attention is poor attention. Multitasking, while still expected and glorified in the corporate world, has been exposed as a myth by modern neuroscience.*

How mindfulness trains attention

One central aspect of mindfulness as well as one of its major benefits is the control of attention. Roughly speaking, we can distinguish between two types of practices:

1 the practice of **focused attention**, which, as the name suggests, focuses attention on a single object, usually the breath
2 **open presence** (also called choiceless awareness) where attention is directed to anything that arises from within or the outside, without preference.

In the beginning we learn to train our attention to stay focused on one particular anchor, most commonly the breath. This practice of focused attention addresses all the challenges to our attention encountered in the workplace, as identified above:

● We train our mind to be able to remain focused on the object of attention for as long as we intend to, as well as notice when it strays from it.
● We learn to deal with external distractions (e.g. noises or sounds in our environment) without losing focus: we simply register them and gently escort our mind back to the breath, without reactivity.
● We manage our internal thirst for more stimulation by committing ourselves to stay focused on the object of attention, without judgement.
● Finally, we learn to shift our attention from one object to another at will (e.g. from our thoughts, emotions, body sensations to the breath and then the body as a whole).

> '*The ability to concentrate on one thing, and not get distracted. There's no point in getting stressed about things you can't control, they key is learning to understand that. It's focusing, and realizing what's important in your business, and not getting distracted by the things that aren't important.*'
>
> Guy Blaskey, CEO of luxury dog-food brand Pooch and Mutt

Practising the art of paying attention in this way will inevitably increase our expertise and skill in doing this, not just while meditating but in real life – and at work. Not only will we perform our roles better but we will be more in touch with the state of our mind and body through paying attention to thoughts and feelings as well as the quality of our breath, thus noticing much earlier than otherwise when we need to take a break, a holiday or even seek help.

Furthermore, the experience of focusing our attention 'on purpose' will make us more conscious of where our attention is placed at any one moment and give us more choices on how we want to deploy this incredible gift mindfully, to serve our business as well as life needs.

TIP *Paying attention is a voluntary act that leads to higher performance, fewer mistakes, less bias, better encoding and sustainable learning.*

Ideas for training mindful attention

● Set your timer on your phone for one minute and form an intention to observe your breath as it unfolds naturally, for the whole duration of the in-breath and the out-breath. If one minute is easy for you, gradually increase the time.

● Using top-down goal-setting and engaging the language centre of your brain, count each full breath (one complete cycle of in-breath and out-breath) until you reach ten breaths, then start over. When your mind wanders and you lose track of your counting, start again.

● Focus your attention on a particular sensation of your breath, wherever you feel it most intensely: the sensation of the cold air coming into your nostrils and the warm air coming out, or the rising and falling of your belly during the breath.

What to try at work:

Whenever you need to work on a particular task requiring focused attention **set an intention** to remain focused on this for the duration of the time you have set aside, consciously letting go of anything else.

When **distractions** occur, **acknowledge** them and consciously decide to deal with them later, if need be.

To prevent yourself looking elsewhere for more stimulation **notice as many features of your current task** as you can. Acknowledge and appreciate all aspects of what you are doing or who you are with.

Be mindful of **where** you focus your attention – if you notice any unhelpful thoughts or comments, make a conscious decision not to dwell on them; instead, gently escort your mind back to whatever you intended to be doing.

Summary

Today we explored why attention is such a crucial skill for the workplace as a way to process information and prevent information overload. Having established selectivity as a common feature of several models of attention we distinguished between goal- and stimulus-driven attention. Subsequently, we identified some of the common challenges on our attention in the workplace.

Further, we dispelled the most common myth around attention and unveiled that there is no such thing as multitasking as information is processed sequentially by our brain. Only undivided or focused attention ensures full encoding of information, which is a prerequisite for sustainable learning. Performance – accuracy as well as speed – is impaired when we multitask.

Lastly, we explored how mindfulness can help us overcome the common challenges to our attention in the workplace by giving us a choice of where to focus our attention and how to sustain it.

SUNDAY

MONDAY

TUESDAY

WEDNESDAY

THURSDAY

FRIDAY

SATURDAY

Fact-check (answers at the back)

1. Attention requires a balancing act between
   a) What to do now and what to do later ❏
   b) The big picture and the detail ❏
   c) Your goals and your tasks ❏
   d) Selecting and inhibiting information ❏

2. Which adjectives best describe attention?
   a) Inexhaustible ❏
   b) Unlimited ❏
   c) Limited and selective ❏
   d) Undiscerning ❏

3. What does top-down information processing mean?
   a) Attending to goal-relevant information ❏
   b) Attending to what the senior management expects ❏
   c) Attending to the big picture rather than the details ❏
   d) Processing information in chronological order ❏

4. The ultimate purpose of stimulus-driven processing is to
   a) Be more mindful ❏
   b) Notice the details in your environment ❏
   c) Keep you interested and engaged ❏
   d) Alert you to events that may be relevant to your survival ❏

5. What is meant by 'dual-task interference'?
   a) Multitasking ❏
   b) When two tasks disturb your working day ❏
   c) The impairment of performance when two tasks are accomplished simultaneously ❏
   d) The preference for one task over another ❏

6. How is attention relevant to learning and memory?
   a) Only information attended to can be encoded and retrieved successfully ❏
   b) You have to pay attention to your memories ❏
   c) You need a good memory in order to learn ❏
   d) If you pay attention, you will enjoy learning more ❏

7. Which mindfulness practice contributes most to overcoming attentional challenges in the workplace?
   a) Open presence ❏
   b) Focused attention ❏
   c) Choiceless awareness ❏
   d) Informal practices ❏

8. What is the main benefit of training our attention?
   a) Overcoming multitasking ❏
   b) Prioritizing the right thing ❏
   c) Better concentration ❏
   d) Giving us more choice about where and how to focus ❏

9. How does training attention affect the brain?
a) It changes it
b) Not at all
c) It makes it smarter
d) It helps it think

10. For which function is attention *not* crucial?
a) Decision-making
b) Performance
c) Learning and memory
d) Teamwork

TUESDAY

Enhancing your performance

In most organizations there is naturally a lot of talk about performance, often at the expense of deeper principles such as meaning, purpose and happiness. Sadly, the overriding preoccupation with performance more often than not seems to be at odds with employees' wellbeing. As a result, and in an effort to maximize performance, managers often push themselves and their teams hard and beyond the call of duty: employees work 12- to 15-hour days, they plough away through weekends or even sleep at the desk, often with disastrous consequences for their own physical, mental and emotional health.

Today we will uncover some of the myths behind performance that companies and employees often fall prey to. Following on from this we will define performance as a state of optimal mental arousal. We will look at the neuroscience of performance and establish which conditions in the brain enable peak performance. You will have the opportunity to explore when and how often you are operating under such conditions and what changes you might want to make to amplify these. Finally, we will share some tips on using mindfulness to help you get 'into the zone' more often.

Myths around performance

There is a myth that is being perpetuated through the ethos of many companies that wish to remain competitive. This myth seems to suggest that increased input will lead to increased output and that performance and productivity are therefore the direct result of the hours you put in. But is this really true? Research has shown that our attention span is exhausted within minutes rather than hours, and that if you do not take regular breaks your brain will eventually take an involuntary break in the form of disturbed attention, leading to errors and bad decisions, as well as ill health. According to an article in the *Harvard Business Review* (Hallowell 2005), this has reached epidemic proportions in today's organizations. Hallowell names this condition, caused by 'brain overload', and accompanied by symptoms such as 'distractibility, inner frenzy, and impatience', as well as 'difficulty staying organized, setting priorities, and managing time', **attention deficit trait** (ADT).

The neuroscience of optimal performance

So how much sense does it make to keep pushing further through the barriers of pain and to defy one's body's and brain's need for a break, food, sleep and overall balance? Not much, according to recent neuroscience research. In fact, you will do yourself some serious damage and compromise your performance along the way.

To help us understand optimal performance it is useful to explore the neuroscience behind it. You may be familiar with the fairy tale of 'Goldilocks and the Three Bears'? Goldilocks needed everything to be 'just right': the porridge she ate, the chair she sat on, the bed she slept in. According to neurobiologist Amy Arnsten (2004), the part of our brain in charge of higher executive functions (decision-making, planning, abstract thinking), the prefrontal cortex (PFC), is the 'Goldilocks of the brain'. It needs a very precise environment of the brain's chemicals (known as neurotransmitters) to function at its best.

This 'sweet spot' of peak performance is easily compromised: as you can see in the inverted U-curve diagram below. If the brain does not release sufficient amounts of noradrenalin and dopamine, we tend to be lethargic and sleepy, unfocused, bored and distracted. This may be the case when you are lacking motivation or have disengaged from your work because you are no longer stimulated or because you may have become disenchanted with your boss, colleagues or other working conditions.

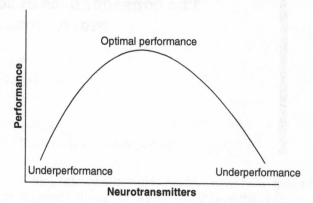

Optimal performance curve

If the neurotransmitters are, on the other hand, over-activated, as is the case with many busy managers and employees in today's fast-paced adrenalin-packed workplace, stress ensues and the brain goes into overdrive. In this over-aroused state, performance of your executive brain is compromised and starts declining rapidly. This can ultimately lead to burnout or cognitive shutdown. **In other words, too much stimulation is just as counterproductive and detrimental to your performance as insufficient chemical arousal.** In order to perform at your personal peak you need to work in alignment with your ideal level of neurotransmitters that regulate your thinking brain.

The consequences of too little mental activation

- Boredom
- Lack of concentration and focus
- Sleepiness, lethargy
- Apathy
- Lack of motivation
- Disengagement

The consequences of too much arousal

- Stress
- Tension
- Restlessness
- Anxiety
- Burnout
- Depression
- Hyper-reactivity to perceived threat

Although the consequences of too little mental arousal look diametrically different from those of too much activation, they have something very fundamental in common:

- They both impair cognitive functioning, memory encoding and retrieval
- They both compromise rational and responsible decision-making
- They both subvert emotional intelligence and regulation
- They both disable healthy relationships.

In short, they severely lower performance.
Conversely, when you hit your sweet spot:

- You are optimally positioned for higher cognitive functioning, goal pursuit, abstract thinking and planning, organizing and communicating

- You find it easier to commit information to memory and remember it later
- You are capable of greater focus, deeper empathy, better impulse control, clearer communication and wiser decision-making.

It is thus essential to maintain an ideal chemical environment for the executive centre to perform at its best, which is something that varies from person to person.

Looking at the inverted U-shape of the optimal performance curve, where would you position yourself overall, 80 per cent of the time? At work, do you tend to be under or over stimulated? Does your position on the arousal curve vary from day to day or from morning, midday to evening? Does it vary according to the task? Depending on the time of the week? Take a moment to write down your insights from your reflections.

The importance of dopamine

As discussed above, the sweet spot of peak performance is hit when the two key neurotransmitters in your PFC, dopamine and noradrenalin, are perfectly in sync. Neurotransmitters are the chemical signals that relay information from neuron to neuron via synapses, the connections between neurons. Communication in the brain is essentially a chemical process.

Dopamine is the key driver of the reward response and is at the heart of any feeling to do with 'approach' states (e.g. motivation, curiosity, interest, desire). The dopamine level also signals the expected reward or pleasure from future events and is therefore a decisive factor in decision-making. Furthermore, dopamine levels also rise with novelty, giving you a rush of dopamine when new connections are formed in the brain. Unsurprisingly, dopamine is therefore one of the key neurotransmitters that is released when people have insights, those euphoric 'eureka' moments. And, lastly, dopamine is central to initiating physical movement.

In the PFC, dopamine is crucial, in conjunction with noradrenalin, for optimal functioning, mental focus and efficiency. Too little can be just as damaging as too much. The PFC needs just the right amount of both neurotransmitters to function at its optimum, as demonstrated in the inverted U-shape of the optimal arousal curve.

As a key excitatory neurotransmitter connected to all approach-related emotional states, dopamine is of central importance to the corporate world in terms of our goal-setting and goal-pursuit capabilities, as well as motivation, learning and the management of expectations.

> *'A few years ago, people took multitasking to be a great virtue. But it's about finding that quiet, centred place within so you're functioning at a much higher level of performance.... It's not just about stress reduction but having a capacity for insight and awareness, and engaging on a whole new level.'*
>
> Qua Veda, Intel

Mindfulness and performance

But how can we empower ourselves to achieve peak performance? This is where mindfulness comes in. While mindfulness naturally takes care of our mental wellbeing, and of all the other benefits outlined in this book, it can also, crucially for the workplace, enhance performance and therefore productivity in several direct and indirect ways.

> *'[Mindfulness] can help employees be more productive and make better decisions for the organization, which helps improve the bottom line of a business. Research from the mindfulness program we now offer to*

all Aetna employees shows that participants are regaining 69 minutes per week of productivity. This increase in productivity equates to an 11:1 return on investment.'

Mark Bertolini, CEO of Aetna

Direct ways of improving performance

- By fostering a wide attentional focus on external phenomena, mindfulness can thus help prevent costly mistakes that occur when employees miss crucial cues in their environment.
- Its external attentional focus enables people to take notice of emotional and social cues from the people they interact with. A field study of trial lawyers showed the key role of mindfulness in permitting lawyers to take into account a wide range of courtroom phenomena, including the facial expressions and reactions of the judge, jury members, and opposing lawyers, which were instrumental for judging when and how to argue their case and employ other persuasive tactics (Dane 2008).
- Mindfulness supports executive functioning, essential for good performance, by aiding clarity of mind. Research has shown that here is a negative relationship between mindfulness and cognitive failures (Herndon 2008).
- In its honing of narrow-focus attention, mindfulness helps sustain focus on the task at hand and block out distractions (see Monday).
- Mindfulness increases employees' attention span, enabling them to work in a focused way for longer.

Indirect ways of improving performance

- Mindfulness reduces stress, which, as we saw on Monday, impairs performance.

- Mindfulness can increase job satisfaction, which is conducive to performance.
- Mindfulness increases general wellbeing – happy workers perform better!
- Mindfulness decreases psychological distress by fostering acceptance – that is, being 'OK with' whatever is happening, facilitating mood-independent performance.
- Mindfulness reduces health-related absenteeism, removing one of the major drains on productivity.

> *'This is a tough economy. Stress reduction and mindfulness don't just make us happier and healthier, they're a proven competitive advantage for any business.'*
>
> Arianna Huffington, founder of the *Huffington Post*

Mindfulness and routine tasks

We all have certain routine tasks at work which we need to do as part of our job description but which do not really excite us as they may be repetitive, mechanical, uninspiring – in short, boring. You may need to do some bookkeeping, log calls, update spreadsheets, compile information, send standardized emails or something similar every day, every week, every month. As we have already seen, 'neurons that fire together, wire together', and the more we repeat a specific task the more it becomes hardwired in a subcortical region of the brain called the basal ganglia. This is where the implicit process of the task is embedded, ensuring that it becomes a habit, something we can do without thinking about it, a bit like riding a bike.

It is extremely useful that the brain is able to form such deep mental grooves through repetition, allowing you to perform this action routinely – that is, on autopilot. It helps conserve precious resources from the energy-intensive prefrontal cortex that does all the thinking.

However, the benefits of this ingenious performance economy in the brain are also its pitfall, which may affect your performance: while you go through the motions with the help of your basal ganglia, giving your easily depleted PFC a break to recharge its batteries, your executive centre goes on annual leave! If your mind is not focusing on the task, lost in thought or daydreaming, mistakes can happen as you may fail to detect slight changes or details, either in the task itself or with something else happening in your immediate environment.

Another caveat is that while you execute something in a perfunctory manner your conscious mind disengages and gets bored, leading to a drop in dopamine, which is also detrimental to your performance, as we have seen.

Optimizing dopamine levels through mindfulness

One of the ways in which mindfulness can help us achieve optimal performance is by regulating and optimizing the dopamine levels in our brain, which are so crucial for the chemical balance in our PFC.

More specifically, dopamine is associated with two essential functions involved in paying attention (see Monday):

1 maintaining focus on the task at hand
2 'updating' the mental sketchpad that is our working memory with new, incoming information, as and when necessary.

A steady supply of this neurotransmitter ensures that the gate to working memory remains firmly closed. This mechanism supports our focus on the task at hand by blocking out any stimuli that may divert our attention. If dopamine levels plunge, or, indeed, if they rise further, this gate to our working memory will open, letting new information enter and throwing us off course.

Thus, the key to keeping the gates to your working memory closed, enabling a steady focus that will keep you operating around your sweet spot of optimal mental arousal, is to ensure that your dopamine supply remains steady and high as much as possible.

One way that mindfulness can help you experience more reward from whatever you are working on is by enabling you to place your full attention on the task at hand – no matter how tedious, tiring or challenging you may find it – and approach it with an attitude of openness, acceptance and curiosity; in other words, with '**beginner's mind**', setting aside any expectations or previous experience you may have. Beginner's mind will serve you by keeping the novelty and hence the reward value of the task high (as novelty is intrinsically rewarding for the brain): by noticing all of its different and hitherto unnoticed aspects and features, as well as any reactions to it that may arise (e.g. resistance, resentment, frustration, boredom, disengagement, as well as tendencies to rush, avoid or resort to doing it mindlessly). Being fully present in mind and body will help you enjoy even the least enjoyable activities – after all, they will not last for ever!

Tips for increasing novelty and reward through beginner's mind at work

Be curious: really notice as many new aspects of what you are doing, no matter how small or insignificant they may seem. Imagine showing and explaining them to a curious child – what would you say to them to engage their attention and interest? Doing this will increase your presence in the moment, make you more alert and increase your enjoyment of the task.

Do things differently: resolve and practise doing things slightly differently from the way you normally would, especially for routine tasks: sit in a different chair or position, possibly in another room, if available, and tackle the task in a new way, as if you have never done it before, even if there seems to be only a subtle difference. This could be about the preparation, the execution or the attitude in your mind. Have fun experimenting with this and operating 'out of character': for example, create a mind map or make a list; use a different font or colour, a different choice of words, greeting, structure or layout; work in a more intuitive or a more linear, sequential way; engage your reason or your emotion more than you normally would in this situation. This unfamiliarity or novelty effect will wake up your executive centre and keep dopamine levels high!

Appreciate: start cultivating an appreciation for the importance of what you are doing, see its necessity and place in the bigger scheme of things, the value it adds to your team, your customers, the organization as a whole or, in a small way, even society at large. As well as increasing your appreciation of your work, this will also make you feel the interconnectedness of all things.

'We have a wellbeing portal on our intranet which provides resources to staff on a range of topics to do with health and wellbeing. These include mindfulness podcasts which we have promoted to staff since May 2014. As an employer we believe improving employees' ability to maintain their health and wellbeing, handle pressure and balance work and home life is commonsense, because ultimately it leads to improved individual and organizational performance.'

A spokesperson for the London Mayor's Office

Summary

Today we uncovered the myth that performance is a direct product of the working hours we invest, proposing instead an inverted U-curve as a more adequate model of performance. We defined performance as a state of optimal mental arousal in the brain's prefrontal cortex, which necessitates a very precise chemical environment of the two key neurotransmitters dopamine and noradrenalin in our executive centre.

We explored the detrimental effects of an under-aroused as well as an over-stimulated brain, which, while bearing different signatures, both lead to a state of underperformance. We then identified direct ways in which mindfulness can help improve performance through both its narrow and its wider attentional focus. We also explored several indirect ways in which mindfulness may enhance performance by reducing some of the factors that can compromise the quality of our work.

We subsequently had a closer look at the role of dopamine and its links to novelty and reward and learned how mindfulness can ensure high and steady levels of this neurotransmitter in support of optimal performance through approaching tasks with 'beginner's mind'. Finally, we shared three practices that will help you embed this approach into your working day.

Fact-check (answers at the back)

1. Which label has been given to the condition of brain overload in organizations?
   a) Attention deficit disorder ❑
   b) Attention deficit trait ❑
   c) ADHD ❑
   d) Performance anxiety ❑

2. Why has our PFC been likened to the fairy-tale character Goldilocks?
   a) It is curious to discover new things ❑
   b) It rules over areas of the brain similar to the three bears ❑
   c) It grabs resources without asking ❑
   d) It needs everything 'just right' ❑

3. What are the brain's chemicals called?
   a) Neurotoxins ❑
   b) Neurons ❑
   c) Neurotransmitters ❑
   d) Neurodegeneration ❑

4. Which two of the following chemicals determine peak performance?
   a) Serotonin ❑
   b) Noradrenalin ❑
   c) Oxytocin ❑
   d) Dopamine ❑

5. If you are to the left of your 'sweet spot', you may be feeling
   a) Alert ❑
   b) Excited ❑
   c) Stressed ❑
   d) Lethargic ❑

6. Over-arousal may lead to
   a) Over-performance ❑
   b) Disengagement ❑
   c) Burnout ❑
   d) Boredom ❑

7. High levels of dopamine are associated with
   a) Insomnia ❑
   b) Attention and motivation ❑
   c) Avoidance ❑
   d) Loss of voluntary movement ❑

8. Which part of the brain is associated with habit formation?
   a) The prefrontal cortex ❑
   b) The amygdala ❑
   c) The basal ganglia ❑
   d) The hippocampus ❑

9. From a brain perspective, what is the purpose of habits?
   a) To strengthen certain connections in the brain ❑
   b) To stimulate your executive centre ❑
   c) To help you perform better ❑
   d) To conserve precious resources of your PFC ❑

10. How can mindfulness help you keep dopamine levels high?
    a) Through the cultivation of beginner's mind ❑
    b) Through relaxing your mind ❑
    c) Through new meditation practices ❑
    d) Through clearing your thoughts ❑

WEDNESDAY

Controlling your stress levels

Stress nowadays seems to be accepted as a natural corollary of corporate life, with a large proportion of all employees considering themselves stressed, a label that has lost its threatening connotations and has almost gained the character of a status symbol. One is expected to have a high threshold for stress, which rises with increasing responsibility and seniority at work. Having said this, thanks to the advances of neuroscience, we are becoming increasingly familiar with the detrimental effects of chronic stress on our health, our brain and our wellbeing.

In this chapter we will explore some facts and figures about the global stress epidemic in the workplace and its concomitant costs to the economy. We will learn what stress means from a brain perspective and what damage it does, explore the origins and physiology of the stress response, and learn how to reduce the stressful activation of the nervous system through mindfulness practice.

What is stress?

Many employees complain about stress. Yet before we look at different ways of reducing our stress levels we need to understand what we mean by stress. There is no clear consensus on this. Stress is a blanket term, widely used, and possibly overused, to describe a wide range of different situations. It is highly subjective and does not present in a uniform manner. Rather, it manifests in many different ways in different people, whose thresholds for what they find stressful also varies strongly.

For the purpose of this book, we propose a working definition of stress as the activation of the mind and the body in response to a situation (whether real or imagined) that is experienced as threatening in some way. It is a mechanism to help the organism cope with challenges or onslaughts to its equilibrium. To be more precise, we can distinguish among the following aspects of stress:

- the stimuli that trigger stress (stressors), classified into different types of stressors
- the individual's subjective feeling of stress (perceived stress)
- stress-related cognitions (e.g. threat appraisal, anxiety, worry, rumination, negative thinking)
- stress arousal (physiological responses).

We will look at what such stressors may be in the workplace and what the stress response entails physically and mentally later in this chapter. First, it is crucial to understand the severity of stress as a major challenge for employees' health and wellbeing and its concomitant cost to organizations.

The extent and cost of workplace stress

Workplace stress has become something of a global epidemic, as evidenced by the following stress-related facts and statistics from around the world, compiled by the Global Organization for Stress (http://www.gostress.com/stress-facts):

- 80 per cent of workers feel stress on the job and nearly half say they need help in learning how to manage stress; 42 per cent say their co-workers need such help (American Institute of Stress).
- Stress levels in the workplace are rising, with six in ten workers in major global economies experiencing increased workplace stress. China (86%) has the highest rise in workplace stress (The Regus Group).
- Australian employees are absent for an average of 3.2 working days each year through stress. This workplace stress costs the Australian economy approximately $14.2 billion (Medibank).
- An estimated 442,000 individuals in Britain, who worked in 2007/08 believed that they were experiencing work-related stress at a level that was making them ill (Labour Force Survey).
- Approximately 13.7 million working days are lost each year in the UK as a result of work-related illness at a cost of £28.3 billion per year (National Institute for Health and Clinical Excellence).

'Mindfulness and yoga-based programs can also help reduce stress, which is a universal issue that can damage people's health. Our research found that employees reporting the highest stress level had nearly $2,000 higher medical costs for the preceding year than those reporting the lowest stress levels. These programs were successfully proven to reduce stress, which can help reduce associated health care costs.'

Mark Bertolini, CEO of Aetna

The neuroscience and physiology of stress

The stress response has its roots in our evolution. Our ancestors needed to ensure their survival and safety from various predators. Over millions of years those individuals who were skilful at fighting, fleeing or freezing in the face of a life-threatening situation passed on this 'fight or flight' response to the next generation. Those who failed to do so perished.

So what happens during stress? When we feel threatened or under pressure in any way, our mind and body are on heightened alert, sounding alarm bells and mobilizing for the fight or flight response. This is executed by the autonomic nervous system (ANS), which regulates our internal organs (viscera) such as the heart, the stomach and the intestines as well as some of our muscles.

'Fight or flight'

There are two parts of the ANS that are of interest in the context of stress: the sympathetic wing and the parasympathetic wing. When we feel stressed, the sympathetic wing of the nervous system (SNS) kicks into action in combination with the hypothalamic–pituitary–adrenal axis, getting you ready to fight that threat!

When you enter fight or flight mode, the thalamus signals to the brain stem to flood your brain with the excitatory neurotransmitter noradrenalin. Your adrenal glands are instructed by the hypothalamus (the brain's controller of the endocrine system) via the pituitary gland to release the stress hormones adrenalin, noradrenalin and the steroid hormone cortisol. This makes your pupils dilate, your heart rate and blood pressure increase, the bronchioles of your lungs enlarge and your digestive system temporarily grind to a halt in order to be able to perform under pressure and fight off the stressor – you need to be able to see better, run faster, breathe more easily and block out any low-priority functions (e.g. digestion) that may get in the way of this battle.

A short-term release of cortisol can be beneficial as it has an anti-inflammatory effect (designed to help heal wounds more quickly), but if it becomes chronic it is detrimental for the immune system and can lead to a decline in the function or structure of brain cells (neurodegeneration), which may ultimately result in neuronal death. Cortisol also stimulates the amygdala, which instigated these changes in the first place, by further ringing the alarm bell, which can lead to hyper-vigilance (an exaggerated sensitization to threat) and further cortisol production. The prefrontal cortex is tipped beyond the sweet spot of optimal performance and becomes severely compromised, as does the hippocampus, which is essential for learning and memory as well as for modulating the amygdala – altogether a toxic combination in terms of healthy functioning.

You can see why such extreme physical and mental reactions are designed as short-term mechanisms against stressors but not as a permanent state of affairs. The problem with our modern-day stress epidemic is that a great proportion of workers are under chronic mild to moderate stress, which takes its toll on the brain and the body, compromising the immune system and cognitive functioning, lowering mood, increasing the risk of depression and leading to emotional hyper-reactivity.

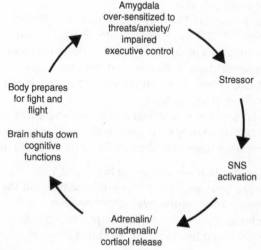

Fight-or-flight cycle

'Rest and digest'

The parasympathetic wing of the ANS works in the opposite way. Also dubbed the 'rest and digest' system, it is active when we are feeling calm, relaxed, happy and safe. With no threats to fight our pupils can constrict, the heart can slow down, the lungs can revert to their normal size and the internal organs can resume their function. This is and should be our default state, albeit somewhat elusive in today's workplace. Let us explore what we can do to redress the balance, bringing both body and mind back into a state of equilibrium.

Social threats – workplace stressors

Nowadays, we are no longer in acute physical danger of being attacked by wild animals – today's threats in the workplace are of a more social kind: our standing within our team may come under threat, our role may be cut, we may feel excluded from our team or department, unfairly treated in the annual bonus round, or not given as much information or control to determine our own workload, job description or working hours. Social threats abound.

As neuroscientists Matthew Lieberman and Naomi Eisenberger (2008) have demonstrated in experiments using fMRI, the networks in our brains that activate in response to physical pain or danger also do so during social pain. As far as our brain is concerned, social threats are as much an issue of life or death as physical ones.

The main areas where stress can be felt and a threat or 'away' response may be triggered at work (as well as elsewhere) have been identified by David Rock (2008) as:

- Status – your place in the social hierarchy
- Certainty – your ability to make predictions about the future
- Autonomy – your control over what happens
- Relatedness – your sense of belonging to a group
- Fairness – being treated in an equitable manner.

These social areas also respond to rewards, in which case they mobilize a sense of 'toward' or approach. However, for reasons we will explore later, threats weigh more heavily than rewards.

Explore which of the five factors trigger the strongest stress response in you by ranking these in order of severity, starting with the strongest:

- Does it bother you most when you feel diminished in your standing at work? (*Status*)
- Do you react with worry, insecurity or even anger when you are not provided with the full picture of what is going on in your team or the organization as a whole? (*Certainty*)
- Is not being in control of your own destiny most stressful to you? (*Autonomy*)
- Do you feel insecure and upset when your sense of belonging and acceptance by others is under threat? (*Relatedness*)
- Are you most bothered when your sense of justice and fairness come under fire? (*Fairness*)

How mindfulness alleviates stress

There is a growing scientific evidence base demonstrating the beneficial effects of mindfulness on cellular, hormonal and immune markers associated with a reduced physiological stress response. In addition, it has been shown to reduce perceived stress, which may be just as important in terms of the distress and detrimental effects on mind and body.

As we explored on Sunday, mindfulness in the West started off as a stress reduction intervention (MBSR) for chronically ill patients and has proven hugely beneficial in managing their distressing symptoms and their perceived stress. Subsequently, several studies in therapeutic contexts (e.g. on cancer patients) have demonstrated a significant reduction in cortisol levels when assessed before and after the MBSR programme. These improvements often proved to be sustainable in the longer term, as participants showed reduced cortisol levels even at the six or twelve-month follow-up (Carlson et al. 2007).

Interestingly, there is also some evidence to suggest that mindfulness may have a positive effect on stress on the cellular level and may play a role in slowing down cellular ageing, as measured by increased telomere length. Telomeres are protective 'caps', stretches of DNA at the end of our chromosomes, which protect our genetic material. Each time a cell divides, telomeres become shorter, until they are so short that cells can no longer divide, leading to cellular death. The shortening of telomeres is associated with ageing, cancer and a higher risk of death.

What makes mindfulness an ideal practice to reduce stress are the following factors:

- Mindfulness practice stimulates the parasympathetic nervous system through its calming emphasis on the breath. Although not primarily aimed at relaxation, relaxation surely is a pleasant and beneficial side effect.
- Activation and sensitization of the fear centre of the brain (amygdala) are drastically reduced.
- The volume of the hippocampus, which can dampen down limbic responses, increases.
- Mindfulness increases bodily awareness (interoception) and mental self-awareness through the close observation of thoughts, feelings and sensations. This alerts us to any stressful activation right from the beginning and gives us a choice on how to deal with it (e.g. by doing more mindfulness!) before we are sucked into the downward spiral of stress reactivity.
- Metacognitive awareness: being aware of the stress signals in your mind and body you are more able to dis-identify from them, holding them in a vast space of awareness, letting them be.

Mindfulness exercises to calm the nervous system on the job

Here are some tips on how you can use mindfulness while you are sitting at your desk to reduce the stressful activation of the nervous system and to stimulate your parasympathetic system:

- Take three calming breaths: breathe in for five counts, breathe out for seven (a longer outbreath has a calming effect).
- Work with a smile: rather than sitting or walking around the office with a grim expression on your face make a habit of smiling. This sends the message to your brain that you are safe and will relax the nervous system as well as induce a state of wellbeing.
- Try laughing out loud at the next mildly funny thing you see or hear (laughter relaxes you and lifts your mood, which also reduces stress levels).
- Indulge yourself with a long yawn, deliberately initiating a relaxed, almost drowsy state.
- Take a mindful minute (or two!) when you are feeling very stressed or anxious.

Summary

Today we explored the ever-present topic of stress in the workplace. We started off by defining what we mean by stress and identified different categories of stress. We established some key facts about the extent and cost of workplace stress globally to quantify its detrimental effect.

Further, we explored what happens during stress in our brain and our body, driven by the sympathetic wing of the autonomic nervous system. We honed in on the damaging effects of too much cortisol on brain cells and the negative stress spiral into which it can escalate. We also identified the antidote to stressful 'fight or flight' activation, which lies within the remit of the 'rest and digest' parasympathetic nervous system.

Subsequently, we explored how stress nowadays plays out in the modern workplace and how mindfulness practice can reduce stressful activation of the nervous system.

Fact-check (answers at the back)

1. What is the original purpose of the stress response?
   a) To alert us to the fact that we are working too hard ❑
   b) To ensure our survival in response to threat ❑
   c) To help us stay competitive ❑
   d) To help us perform better ❑

2. Which system in the body is responsible for the stress response?
   a) The central nervous system ❑
   b) The digestive system ❑
   c) The cardiovascular system ❑
   d) The autonomic nervous system ❑

3. When we are stressed we activate the
   a) Sympathetic nervous system ❑
   b) Parasympathetic nervous system ❑
   c) Prefrontal cortex ❑
   d) Blood pressure ❑

4. Which of the following hormones is not associated with stress?
   a) Cortisol ❑
   b) Noradrenalin ❑
   c) Adrenalin ❑
   d) Testosterone ❑

5. What is the effect of too much stress on executive function?
   a) It stimulates thinking and performance ❑
   b) It impairs performance ❑
   c) It has no impact ❑
   d) It increases alertness ❑

6. Cortisol can lead to
   a) Neuroregeneration ❑
   b) Neurotoxicity ❑
   c) Neurodegeneration ❑
   d) Inflammation ❑

7. Why can social factors trigger a fight or flight response?
   a) Social situations are naturally threatening ❑
   b) They may compromise your safety ❑
   c) You may be hypersensitive ❑
   d) Social threats activate the same brain networks as physical threats ❑

8. Which social need can trigger threat?
   a) Competence ❑
   b) Certainty ❑
   c) Comprehension ❑
   d) Creativity ❑

9. Evidence of telomere lengthening suggests that mindfulness
   a) May contribute to better genetic material ❑
   b) May contribute to a better immune system ❑
   c) May counteract cellular ageing ❑
   d) May contribute to a more youthful look ❑

10. How does mindfulness reduce the stress response?
    a) By stimulating the parasympathetic nervous system ❑
    b) By triggering the sympathetic nervous system ❑
    c) By avoiding the triggers of stress ❑
    d) By facing up to the causes of stress ❑

THURSDAY

Regulating your emotions

Contrary to the prevalent ethos of many companies and corporate executives, organizations are emotional hot houses. It is neither realistic to leave your emotions at home when you come to work, nor should you have to. Emotions are a normal and even desirable part of working life and an integral, enabling part of decision-making, professional or otherwise – but they need to be managed. Unfortunately, more often than not, emotions are managed poorly and relationships at work can be just as dysfunctional as they may be beyond the workplace.

In this chapter we will look at the two ways the brain processes emotions – the fast and automatic way of emotional reactivity and the slow and considered way of emotion regulation – explore different emotion regulation strategies and introduce you to mindfulness as an alternative and constructive way of managing how you feel. We will review the current evidence from neuroscience on mindfulness as an emotion regulation strategy, which can help us manage emotions from the top down and from the bottom up. To conclude, drawing on Buddhist wisdom on emotions we will learn how to 'sit' with emotions in a mindful way, allowing them to arise without reactivity.

Emotional processing: low road or high road?

So, what are emotions and why are they so important? Literally meaning 'movements', emotions originate in physical sensations and can be described as responses to internal or external events, which are of particular significance to the individual. According to neuroscientist Antonio Damasio, emotions are an important part in the organism's equilibrium and intimately related to reward and punishment mechanisms. They both represent and regulate the body state. Emotions occur automatically and change the body, brain and mental state in profound ways.

Emotions have a huge impact in the workplace, just as everywhere else. They affect employees'

● mood and attitude
● wellbeing
● stress levels
● productivity
● performance
● working relationships
● decision-making
● job satisfaction

No employee or executive can afford to ignore their emotions (or other people's, for that matter) or take them lightly. Scientists have distinguished two distinct pathways of processing emotions in the brain, which have been dubbed the low road versus the high road of emotional expression.

Steps involved in emotional processing

As can be seen in the diagram below, emotions arise in response to a specific event or stimulus. It is our assessment of this stimulus – which may be more or less conscious – that ultimately leads to the emotional response. This response may be regulated to a larger or lesser degree.

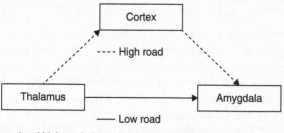

The low road and high road of emotional processing

As it is essentially a stress response, the **low road** of emotional expression is the 'fight or flight' response we explored yesterday, also known as emotional reactivity, 'acting out' or 'mindless emoting' (Teasdale 1999). As discussed, this involves the direct route between the thalamus that receives the input and the amygdala as the seat of emotional reactions. In this pathway, emotions are activated before our cognitive faculties have a chance to intervene and regulate (Wager 2003). Being a short cut in the brain, this route is fast and automatic, requiring no conscious effort.

The **high road** is that of emotion regulation. Here, the thalamus acts as the sensory gateway to the cortex, which orchestrates higher cognitive processes, thus enabling emotion regulation from the top down. As we will see in the next section, such regulation can take different forms. Emotional regulation from the top down is slower as it constitutes an indirect pathway and, as such, it requires considerable conscious mental effort. Emotions can be down-regulated to lessen the impact of negatively perceived stimuli or up-regulated to increase the impact of positive ones.

Emotional regulation strategies

There are a number of different ways to regulate emotions in order to avoid mindless emoting. As the executive centre and the limbic system work in a kind of seesaw effect, where activation of one suppresses the other, we can use insights into emotion regulation to help ourselves get a grip on our amygdala.

Limiting exposure

A proactive way of regulating emotions is to intervene *before* strong and predictable emotions arise in the first place: limit your exposure to situations that elicit threat responses, and avoid, if possible, those that you already know will make you 'go limbic'. For example, if you keep volunteering to present at meetings and then you drive yourself crazy with stage fright you may decide not to keep putting yourself through this.

Tips to try

- Be discerning about what additional workload you take on.
- Only expose yourself to challenges you will benefit from tackling.
- Avoid taking on last-minute commitments.
- Schedule meetings well in advance.
- Set realistic deadlines.
- Avoid exposure to dysfunctional working relationships.
- Choose to work more closely with colleagues with whom you have a better working relationship.

Adjusting exposure

When situations cannot be entirely avoided, which will often be the case in a corporate environment, you may be able to tweak certain aspects in order to avoid strong emotional reactions and ensure maximum 'safety', convenience, flexibility and certainty for yourself or the other people involved.

Tips to try

- Keep your cool by preparing yourself well in advance for meetings.
- Exercise any freedom you may have about setting the time/day/length/agenda of a meeting.

● Make sure that you have some refreshments/snack before any important or emotionally charged decisions, meetings, encounters to avoid low blood sugar or hunger throwing you off course.

Attention focusing

When you come across situations that can neither be avoided nor adjusted you still have an important choice: to decide where to place your attention. You do not have to let yourself be hijacked by maladaptive emotions that make you miserable. Train yourself to focus your attention on *other* aspects of the situation, constructive outcomes, positive features, any consensus within your team, rather than remain stuck in negativity bias. Before important events or situations, prime your brain to pay attention to positive aspects and outcomes. As we have seen, directing your attention on purpose is a crucial skill and focus of mindfulness.

Verbal labelling

Neuroimaging studies have shown that the act of verbal labeling – that is, attaching a name to an affective state – can help down-regulate emotional processes through the activation of the right ventro-lateral part of your PFC, which exerts an inhibitory function on the amygdala, dampening down limbic responses (Creswell et al. 2007).

Cognitive reappraisal

In this emotion regulation strategy you consciously manipulate the *input* into what is called the emotion-generative system from the top down, again using the executive centre of your brain. Here, you actively reinterpret emotional stimuli in a way that modifies their emotional impact. An example of this would be when you reframe some disappointing feedback to a piece of work in the light of the opportunity for self-improvement that it presents. Functional neuroimaging studies have shown that during reappraisal prefrontal regions of the brain were active while the amygdala showed decreased activation (Ochsner 2008). Similar to verbal labelling, reappraisal down-regulates and inhibits the limbic system.

Suppression

Suppression is a regulation strategy that suppresses the behavioural *output* of the emotion-generative system from the top down. By contrast to cognitive reappraisal, which leads to decreases in limbic area activity, suppression may diminish the acting out of negative emotions but studies have found increased activation of the brain's emotional centre in the long term. While you may be able to prevent acting out your negative emotional experience for a short while, suppression is not a good idea in the long run as it will come at the cost of greater emotional turmoil later.

Managing emotions mindfully: top-down versus bottom-up processing

If you want to handle your emotions in a more constructive way, mindfulness may well be your best bet. There is substantial scientific evidence that, the more you practise, mindfulness will lead to more effective emotion regulation and reduced emotional reactivity. Neuroscientists have found that long-term mindfulness practitioners show less activation and sensitization in limbic regions such as the amygdala. Practitioners learn an alternative way of relating to present-moment experience where both pleasant and unpleasant emotions are allowed to surface but are not acted or dwelled upon with habitual reactivity. Instead, practitioners are encouraged to accept how they feel with self-compassion and be curious about the bodily manifestation of the emotion. This is reflected in the increased activation of the insula, which tracks sensory experiences and thus enables a more vivid and direct experience of reality through the senses while emotions are kept in check.

A review of existing neuroimaging studies by Chiesa et al. (2013) suggests a distinction between novice practitioners who are undergoing initial mindfulness training (e.g. an eight-week MBSR course) and experienced long-term practitioners with several years of regular practice under their belt: while meditation novices tend to display more top-down activation, mindfulness experts show an increased ability to regulate their emotions without the involvement of executive brain areas, thus requiring less conscious effort. This suggests that the more you practise, the less you need to work on actively regulating your emotions, and the more you will become adept at managing your emotions non-cognitively and from the bottom up.

To sum up: mindfulness enables more adaptive emotional processing and the switch from emotional reactivity to emotional responsiveness in a way that can become second nature with increasing practice and skill.

> *'[Meditation] gives me a centeredness, it gives me an ability to look at things without the emotional hijacking, without the ego, in a way that gives me a certain clarity.'*
>
> Ray Dalio, Bridgewater Associates

Try this: mental noting and depersonalizing

When you start off on the mindfulness path, it can be extremely useful to practise top-down regulation. A traditional way of doing this in the light of the evidence on affective labelling presented above, is to engage in a practice, common in the 'insight' meditation tradition, called **mental noting.** When you notice feelings coming up for you, make a soft mental note of what is arising: for

example 'There is anger/disappointment/irritation etc.'
Do not spend too much time trying to identify the right
word and getting embroiled in semantics. The effect of
this practice is that you engage the executive centre of
your brain, which, through the seesaw effect mentioned
above, attenuates the limbic centre, dampening down the
emotional charge of the feeling.

Taking the self out of the equation (by favouring noting such
as 'there is frustration', rather than 'I feel frustrated'), you
also depersonalize the feeling and thus make it less salient
to yourself and your survival – a subconscious fear that is
often triggered when we experience negative feelings, which
then activates the stress response. The key to using this
technique effectively is to keep the label neutral and short
so that you are not taken hostage by the emotion or become
too emotionally involved with it.

A Buddhist perspective

How do experienced mindfulness practitioners manage their
emotions without resorting to either mindless emoting or
cognitive control from the top down? The answer lies within the
foundations of Buddhist philosophy, a brief foray into which will
provide a context for an alternative perspective on emotions
than we are used to in Western societies.

Emotions as passing phenomena

Unlike in Western psychology where emotions are taken
extremely seriously and tend to be seen as integral to who we
are and what defines us, Buddhist philosophy does not attach
the same importance to emotions. Here, emotions are seen as
mental phenomena that arise and fade away just like anything
else, for example thoughts. They have their origin in bodily
sensations and have ultimately no real substance or defining
power over us. Buddhism explicitly warns against constructing
an identity out of our transient emotions as it does not believe
in a stable and separate self in the sense that we tend to do in

the West, where we become so identified with, say, our anger, that we are completely consumed by it, unable to distinguish ourselves from it. In other words, in Buddhism, you are not your emotions – your anger, your disappointment, your sadness – but can, and should, dissociate from them, holding them in a vast space of awareness.

The 'feeling tone' of experience

Yet Buddhism does not deny the existence of emotions, nor their power. Quite the contrary, it encourages allowing and accepting them as they are, but without becoming sucked into them, and proposes three ways of describing what it calls the 'feeling tone' of each experience, classifying it as either pleasant, unpleasant or neutral. So far, so good. There is nothing wrong with experiencing situations or feelings as having a positive or negative emotional valence. The problem only arises once you start *reacting* to a pleasant feeling tone with wanting or clinging and to unpleasant feeling tones with aversion. This grasping for the pleasant and pushing away of the unpleasant creates and perpetuates suffering, due to the ever-changing nature of our experience.

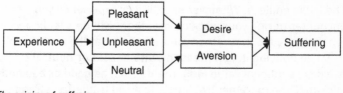

The origins of suffering

Mindfulness practice for emotion regulation

Before we have a go at a four-step practice for working with feelings mindfully, let us have a look at what each of the steps involves and what it does. This process will help you manage your emotions more constructively, and increasingly from the bottom up, the more you practise.

1 Take notice of the feeling tone

The first step towards regulating your emotions is to become more aware of them. This may sound obvious but we often do not notice the initial stirrings of an emotion until it has snowballed into a personal drama, catastrophe or other emotional roller coaster. Make a habit out of registering the emotional charge of all stimuli you encounter during your working day. Here's a checklist to help you get started but do add your own situations or emotional trigger points to it.

How do you feel when...

- you first walk into your office in the morning?
- you walk out of the door in the evening?
- You see or talk to your boss/colleagues/direct reports?
- You sit in a meeting?
- You interact with clients/other stakeholders?
- You meet with a challenge or difficult situation?
- You are working to a deadline?
- Your workload is overwhelming?
- You go on your lunch break?
- You do not have time to take a break?

The list is endless. Whatever situation or experience you encounter during your working day, there will be a feeling tone attached to it, whether you realize that at the time or not. Practise noticing it. **Is it pleasant, unpleasant or neutral?** Avoid conventional value judgements such as good or bad and stick to these more neutral labels to avoid triggering strong likes and dislikes. This part of the exercise is merely about strengthening the power to *notice* the nature of experience as having a specific feeling tone *before* a cascade of emotions are set in motion and hold you hostage.

2 Label your feelings

The second step involves applying a mental label to your emotions by using just one or two words. Here are some examples to help you get started:

- anticipation
- frustration
- excitement
- anger
- trepidation
- satisfaction
- fear
- resentment

- worry
- anxiety
- stress
- elation
- relief
- joy
- pride.

Again, the list goes on. Feel free to add to it and choose the labels that most accurately describe what you feel. Caveat: this is not about 'getting it right' or finding the most accurate description, it is about the power of awareness. Remember to take yourself out of the equation. Rather than 'owning' the feelings, as we are encouraged to do in Western culture, see yourself as the witness, the observer of whatever arises.

3 Allow yourself to feel your feelings

The third step is about allowing yourself to feel whatever arises. As we have seen, regulating emotions mindfully is not about avoiding or suppressing them; it is about changing your attitude or relationship to them: allowing them to arise and fade without reacting to them, whether that is wishing them away or chasing after them.

Now comes the crucial step, the one that will help you get out of the relentless wheel of emotional reactivity and help you process emotions from the bottom up: rather than reacting to your emotions in your usual, habitual way, 'drop' into your body – where do you feel it? Is there a lump in your throat? A queasy feeling in your belly? Does your heart pound? Is your head throbbing? Do you have butterflies in your stomach? A heavy weight on your chest? Bring to this investigation a sense of openness, acceptance and curiosity, and, most importantly, do not judge yourself for feeling what you feel. Practise consciously suspending your value judgements. Tell yourself that it is OK to feel like this, liking or disliking your experience; there is no need to censor it in any way, let alone judge yourself. Your experience is your experience. Yet there is no need to invest any energy in perpetuating, fighting or chasing such feelings. For better or worse, they will arise and pass on their own, much more quickly than you might wish (in the case of the pleasant ones) and much more slowly than you fear (in the case of the unpleasant ones)! So when you explore your feelings, try noticing as many details as possible, focusing on the sensations inside and outside of your body and mentally record them like an impartial scientist would record his or her findings.

4 Dis-identify from your feelings

The last step is crucial. It has to do with the fact that emotions, like all other phenomena, are transient – they come, they go, and you may even come to wonder how you could possibly have felt a certain way only an hour later. How could I have got so worked up about something that does not seem so bad right now? Was it really worth going out of my way to run after this award? While it is important to experience your feelings fully when they arise, it is also vital not to take them for something more substantial or permanent than what they are. Do not get too attached to them. Your emotions are nothing but momentary, situational representations of your physical and mental responses to certain events. You do not have to construct an identity for yourself out of what and how you feel at any one time.

Look at the following train of thought that may snowball from a feeling of fear: 'I am so scared of this presentation, I'm no good at public speaking, nobody will take me seriously, I'm such a loser.' This is as unnecessary as it is dysfunctional, yet many of us will indulge in such faulty reasoning as part of our daily emotional routine. A better way of relating to such emotions, especially the unpleasant ones, is to notice them in an impersonal way. 'Ah, there is anxiety again, rearing its ugly head' or simply 'I notice frustration.' This holds emotions at bay, forcing them to keep their distance, and takes yourself out of the equation. Emotions are just phenomena that arise, not your personal creation. They can lose their power to threaten you and throw you off course. They are nothing more than changing neural weather formations.

> *"Meditation is not about thinking about nothing," he said. "It's about accepting what you think, giving reverence to it and letting it go. It's losing the attachment to it. Same thing with pain."*
>
> Mark Bertolini, CEO of Aetna

Try this!

To help you manage your emotions mindfully, have a go at the following practice on a regular basis, particularly if you are suffering from strong emotional reactivity, triggered by specific, recurrent situations. First of all, spend a few minutes reflecting on what your personal triggers are: What are the things that drive you crazy? What gets your blood boiling? Set an intention to do this practice every time you encounter these.

1 **Notice** the feeling tone: categorize the situation/event as pleasant, unpleasant or neutral. You may find that there are many more neutral events than you ever thought!

2 **Label** your feelings as and when they arise. Practise finding short and snappy adjectives for what you feel ('concerned', 'anxious', 'cheerful'). Do not spend too long worrying about finding the best possible description; this step is about acknowledging your feelings rather than diagnosing them with clinical precision!

3 **Allow** your feelings without judgement. Tell yourself gently 'It is OK to feel like this; no need to judge or do anything about it.' Avoid the temptation to react by fighting pleasant feelings or rejecting those you find unpleasant.

4 **Dis-identify** from your feelings, be careful not to get sucked into them and any drama that may be brewing under the surface. You are not your feelings!

You can practise this both formally, in a moment of calm at home, and also informally when the situation arises. When you practise it on a chair or cushion at home, just see what emotions come up and work with these. The more you practise formally, the stronger your non-reactivity muscles will become and the better you will be able to nip any strong reactions in the bud.

'Between stimulus and response there is a space.
In that space is our power to choose our response.
In our response lies our growth and our freedom.'

Viktor Frankl, Austrian neurologist

Summary

Today we discussed the nature of emotions and their importance in the workplace. We learned about two distinct ways of emotional processing – the fast, automatic and energy-saving 'low road' of amygdala reactivity to a stimulus versus the slower, conscious, energy-consuming 'high road' where emotions are processed via the executive centre of the brain.

We explored a number of different emotion regulation strategies including the two top-down strategies of verbal labelling and cognitive reappraisal that both involve executive control via the PFC. We also discussed suppression as a counterproductive strategy.

Furthermore, we explored neuroimaging findings suggesting that with growing expertise mindfulness practitioners shift from actively managing their emotions from the top down to an increasingly bottom-up regulation without cognitive intervention. We learned from Buddhist philosophy how emotions can lead to suffering to help us understand how mindfulness can

SUNDAY
MONDAY
TUESDAY
WEDNESDAY
THURSDAY
FRIDAY
SATURDAY

support emotion regulation. In addition, we shared the techniques of mental noting and depersonalizing emotions. You were then introduced to a four-step practice for working with emotions that will over time help you regulate them from the bottom up.

Fact-check (answers at the back)

1. Which of the following statements is *not* true about emotions?
   a) Emotions occur automatically ☐
   b) Emotions arise from conscious thinking ☐
   c) Emotions reflect and regulate the state of the body ☐
   d) Emotions occur in response to internal and external events ☐

2. The low road of emotional processing is also called
   a) Mindfulness ☐
   b) Rest and digest ☐
   c) Emotion regulation ☐
   d) Mindless emoting ☐

3. The high road of emotional processing occurs via the
   a) Amygdala ☐
   b) Prefrontal cortex ☐
   c) Thalamus ☐
   d) The limbic system ☐

4. In what way is attention key to emotion regulation?
   a) It helps you focus on the emotions ☐
   b) It strengthens your attentional capacities ☐
   c) It inhibits negative emotions ☐
   d) It gives you the choice not to dwell on unhelpful emotions ☐

5. How does verbal labelling help regulate emotions?
   a) By reappraising them ☐
   b) By amplifying them ☐
   c) By dampening down the amygdala ☐
   d) By suppressing them ☐

6. Why should you be cautious about using suppression as an emotion regulation strategy?
   a) It eventually backfires ☐
   b) It makes you repressed ☐
   c) It is cathartic to act your emotions out ☐
   d) It is maladaptive ☐

7. In what way is mindfulness a bottom-up strategy?
   a) It does not require cognitive intervention ☐
   b) It activates the amygdala ☐
   c) It allows you to identify with your emotions ☐
   d) It does not suppress emotions ☐

8. Which aspect of their emotional experience do mindfulness practitioners tend to focus on?
   a) How it affects their executive centre ☐
   b) The moral ramifications ☐
   c) The deeper meaning of the emotion ☐
   d) The sensations in the body ☐

9. How does mental noting help alleviate painful experiences?
   a) By 'owning' your emotions ☐
   b) By identifying exactly what they are ☐
   c) By depersonalising them ☐
   d) By using language to capture their meaning ☐

10. In Buddhist thinking, suffering is created by
    a) Negative emotions ☐
    b) Reacting to emotions with desire or aversion ☐
    c) The feeling tone of experience ☐
    d) Immoral emotions ☐

FRIDAY

Mindful decision-making

Decision-making is a key part of corporate life. Each employee from a junior clerk to a senior executive is faced with numerous opportunities for decision-making on a daily basis. The higher the rank, the more momentous and far-reaching the decision is likely to be. Often, it is only when decisions incur disastrous consequences that we are alerted to the significance of decision-making in the workplace.

In this chapter we will review some of the underlying causes of unethical workplace behaviour, outline the key components of major decision-making models and explore why and how mindfulness can enhance ethical decision-making. Finally, we will offer some suggestions for using mindfulness to support ethical decision-making, which can pave the way towards more considered and socially responsible corporate behaviour.

Unethical decision-making in the workplace

KPMG Forensic's latest Integrity Survey (2013) into corporate fraud and misconduct, based on the experiences and perceptions of more than 3,500 US employees across all industries, demonstrated that unethical behaviour and misconduct in the workplace are shockingly widespread. According to the survey, 73 per cent of all employees nationally reported that they had observed misconduct in the 12-month period preceding the research. Moreover, 56 per cent of participants stated that what they had witnessed could cause 'a significant loss of public trust if discovered'. This prevalence of unethical behaviour holds true across industries, ranging from 61 per cent in the Media & Communications sector to 82 per cent in the Consumer Market sector (with Banking roughly in the middle at 71 per cent) and makes bleak reading.

Alarmingly, this percentage has risen by 10 per cent since the previous survey in 2009, driven largely by a staggering 26-per-cent increase in reported unethical behaviour in the Electronics, Software and Services industry, followed by a 20-per-cent rise in Consumer Markets and in Chemicals and Diversified Industrials, a 19-per-cent increase in Aerospace and Defence, a 15-per-cent rise in Real Estate and Construction and a 14-per-cent rise in Banking and Financials.

The nature of the specific misconduct, ranging from issues of financial reporting fraud, to a broader set of potential misconduct, was split into 42 different types of offences, distributed among six broad categories of fraud and misconduct, deemed to compromise trust on many levels and affecting different groups, spanning customer or market place trust, supplier trust, shareholder/organizational trust, public or community trust, employee trust or general trust.

Ironically, when asked, employees reported that they were reasonably familiar (77–78%) with the acceptable standards of conduct, as outlined in policies, laws and regulations specific to the employees' job function, as well as the organizational code, values and principles. They also gave positive feedback (over 90%) on the communication and training employees received with regards to those standards.

So what causes employees to act unethically? According to the KPMG survey, the most commonly reported cause was pressure to meet business targets (64%), and, in fact, another three causes were tightly related to this organizational emphasis on meeting targets: the belief that achieving results was rewarded above the means to achieve them (59%), the fear of losing their job if they failed to meet targets (59%) and the lack of resources to get the job done without resorting to unethical means (57%). Selfish motives of self-advancement and disregard for ethical standards played a smaller part in such behaviour (49%).

Ethical traps

A deeper analysis of these and other ethical entanglements that employees and managers of organizations can get caught in have been outlined by Hoyk and Hersey in *The Ethical Executive* (2010), which identifies 45 psychological traps (including biases, justifications and conflicts of interest) that might distort managers' perceptions and entrap them in unethical behaviour that may subvert their desire and intention to act ethically. The authors distinguish between primary traps that are mainly external stimuli that can derail us, defensive traps, which constitute mental manoeuvres to deal with the shame and guilt that ethical transgressions cause us, and personality traps, which are internal traits that make us more prone to wrongdoing.

Evidence also suggests that unethical actions may be caused by self-delusion as a result of subconscious and automatic psychological or cognitive processes, including biases and rationalisations (Carlson et al. 2002). What makes matters worse is the fact that, according to Epley and Caruso (2004), self-serving judgements are effortless and almost immediate, in contrast to effortful and time-consuming perspective-taking, required to develop an unbiased opinion. In addition, Chugh et al. (2005) argue that people have a favourable view of themselves as moral and are often unable to appreciate the extent of their own biases and conflicts of interest, which makes them unable to overcome them.

Moreover, research has established that employees might at times violate their own moral framework in order to fit in with their company's culture. Due to the impact of group and organizational cultures, staff are frequently oblivious to the impact that group pressure may be having on their behaviour. The motivation for unethical acts is often driven by social factors such as conformism (Asch 1951), the impact of authority (Milgram 1963) and social roles (Zimbardo 1974), as well as by group thinking, bystander apathy and dispersed responsibility, among other factors.

In a nutshell, it looks as though, when it comes to acting ethically, we are completely up against it, with a plethora of threats and dangers lurking around us as well as inside us to throw us off course.

Mindfulness and decision-making

As we have established, what is expected of you as employees or managers in the service of corporate profitability may at times be at odds with your own ethical imperatives, disconnecting you from your true intentions and values. By drawing attention to such discrepancies between people's values and their behaviour at work mindfulness, can facilitate moral convergence through its facilitation of insight and direct experience.

Moreover, it is crucial to understand that, although this is not part of its narrow definition, mindfulness needs to be more than just attention training, if one wishes to honour the origins and spirit of its ancient tradition. In its Buddhist context, mindfulness is embedded in a whole system of philosophy and ethics, and constitutes only one part, albeit an important one, of what is called the Noble Eightfold Path, which the Buddha realized at his enlightenment. This path, which is postulated to lead to happiness, includes elements that enable the attainment of wisdom, ethical conduct and mental discipline. While 'right mindfulness' (together with 'right effort' and 'right concentration'] is listed as one of the three attributes facilitating mental discipline, ethics is taken care of by 'right speech', 'right action' and' right livelihood'. In other words, when looking at ethical decision-making, mindfulness needs to be steered in the right direction by our values and virtues. Without these, mindfulness is a like a ship without a rudder.

Mindfulness encourages socially responsible behaviour

Research by INSEAD has shown that traditional executive training approaches, based on cognitive moral reasoning and didactic top-down teaching, are not effective in increasing the likelihood of 'socially responsible behaviour' (SRB; Schneider et al. 2005) in corporates, as they have little or no impact on the three psychological attributes that enable such behaviour: first, the cognitive capacities, manifest in, among others things, moral reasoning and decision-making; second, personal values and, third, emotional dispositions. There is, however, compelling evidence that non-cognitive interventions such as introspection and meditation practices have a significant positive impact on SRB and can succeed in shifting psychological traits and changing personal values towards an increased level of social consciousness among corporate executives (Zollo et al. 2007).

Awareness is key to decision-making

Recent research has indeed demonstrated a strong relationship between mindfulness and ethical decision-making. Mindfulness, in its key sense of being attentive to and aware of one's current experience or present reality (Brown & Ryan 2003), can be seen as a central element of the ethical decision-making process, as illustrated by various decision-making models where awareness of an ethical issue constitutes the crucial first step in a four-stage process (Rest 1986; Jones 1991) before moral reasoning/judgement, forming an intention and taking action can follow:

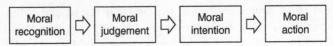

The four-stage process of ethical decision-making

Emotional awareness is thus integral to ethics and has been advocated as an essential contributor to enhanced clarity in ethical decision-making.

A 2010 study by the Wharton Risk Management and Decision Processes Center has established that the correlation between mindfulness and ethical decision-making manifests in three ways: according to self-report measurement scales, mindful individuals are more likely

● to act ethically
● to value upholding ethical standards
● to use a principled approach to ethical decision-making.

In addition, the researchers also found that more mindful individuals cheated less in a behavioural experiment on unethical behaviour.

How mindlessness can promote unethical behaviour

The same study on the impact of mindfulness on ethical awareness and ethical decision-making also demonstrates how a lack of mindfulness can compound various causes of unethical behaviour, for example through what Tenbrunsel and Messick have called 'ethical fading' (2004): in the presence of certain cues in the environment (for example, when they feel observed by a surveillance system, ironically installed to safeguard ethical behaviour) people may lose sight of the ethical dimensions of their actions, and start reframing their decisions as business decisions rather than ethical ones. In such situations, people tend to deceive themselves by the use of justifications and euphemisms in order to protect themselves from facing up to their unethical actions.

Another example is Bandura's model of 'moral disengagement' (1999), where individuals disengage from their moral convictions and justify unethical behaviour by using various strategies to abnegate responsibility and to make their actions palatable to themselves. This process operates below the level of conscious awareness and is hence also exacerbated by a lack of mindfulness.

How mindfulness supports ethical decision-making

But what are the mechanisms by which mindfulness may further ethical decision-making? The pathways via which mindfulness may have a beneficial influence on the decision-making process are outlined below:

Allowing and non-judging lead to less censoring of uncomfortable truths

Mindfulness encourages openness to whatever arises in the mind, including difficult thoughts and emotions that may be potentially detrimental or threatening to one's self-image. For example, if your ego is dented by the fact that your sales record this month has not been up to the expected standard, this painful truth can be held in mindful awareness, overcoming the need to avoid, suppress or mask it. This accepting, non-judging quality of mindfulness can help us be more willing to consider all – even those personally uncomfortable or inconvenient – ethical aspects of a decision rather than find strategies to avoid, ignore or justify them. In this way, mindfulness helps us face up to the possibly more challenging aspects of all ethical considerations and can heighten moral awareness.

Metacognitive awareness and honesty reduce self-delusion

The type of self-awareness honed through mindfulness encompasses awareness of one's own thoughts (metacognitive awareness), which in turn can help curtail unethical behaviour by leading to an increasing dis-identification from one's thinking. Practitioners learn to observe their thoughts increasingly as mental events without becoming embroiled in the story created by their thinking. A common analogy used to illustrate the nature of thoughts is to see them as 'clouds in the sky'; no matter whether they are white and fluffy or dark and menacing, all clouds are ultimately insubstantial in nature and impermanent, destined to arise and pass away. The sky of one's mind, however, or pure awareness, always remains blue, untainted by whatever weather formation may arise at any given moment. This type of metacognitive awareness may thus heighten one's recognition of any deluded or self-serving judgements on ethically ambiguous situations, thereby reducing both their occurrence (to some extent) and their hold over one's mind, opening up a choice of whether to act on them or not. In this way, mindfulness may inhibit unethical behaviour. Research has indeed established that those high in mindfulness value honesty and integrity more highly than external rewards and may thus be more likely to act ethically.

Internal focus can raise alarm bells

Highly mindful individuals tend to be strongly in touch with their current internal experience, closely observing their thoughts, emotions and body sensations. They are hence more likely to notice their internal 'alarm bells', alerting them to the fact that something does not feel right because it may be at odds with their personal values. As a result this internal focus encourages greater alignment with their moral compass. This has indeed been borne out by recent, hitherto unpublished research I and colleagues conducted in the workplace, following a short mindfulness induction.

Being mode

Just as we make a shift from the so-called doing mode towards the domain of 'being' with increasing mindfulness practice, the emphasis of decision-making also moves from the preoccupation with reaching a swift outcome to the increased importance of the process itself. With mindfulness one is more inclined to take one's time and consider the decision carefully and consciously rather than rushing towards making it, while falling prey to the many pitfalls inherent in decision-making. Mindfulness thus minimizes the risk of 'the end justifies the means' type of reasoning, a frequent contributing factor to unethical behaviour.

Compassion

Compassion, also known as loving kindness, is a practice that often goes hand in hand with mindfulness, although it is not strictly speaking part of it. Based on a belief in the connectedness of all creatures (as it includes the animal world, too), who are all linked in their desire to be happy and free from suffering, this practice facilitates perspective-taking and connecting with others, not just with the people close to us but also with those we tend to overlook or ignore and even with potentially 'difficult' people whom we may otherwise dehumanize in our minds. In this way, by making us mindful of our shared humanity, compassion practice can substantially reduce the likelihood of us acting in ways that harm others and thus promote more ethical decision-making.

Emotion regulation

As we saw on Thursday, mindfulness lets us reduce or overcome the automaticity in our reactions, leading to less proneness to short-circuiting (taking the low road) and impulsive decision-making out of anger, revenge or just habit, while being more conducive to emotion regulation, both from the top down (which includes moral reasoning) and, more importantly, from the bottom up, from an increasing ability to practise non-reactivity and mindful choice.

Try this: acting out of virtue

There are two aspects to the concept of virtue, on the one hand refraining from causing harm, both to yourself as well as others, and, on the other hand, actively promoting positive values.

1 Bring to mind some key words or phrases that sum up the virtues you wish to live by.

2 Notice what these feel like in your body by letting them sink into your heart. How does it feel in your body to 'act with integrity', to 'be compassionate' or whatever else you chose as your virtue? Do not *think* about these concepts – just connect with how they *feel* physically and emotionally from the inside.

3 Choose one of your virtues and visualize what would happen if you acted by this precept at all times, irrespective of other people's behaviours. What would happen if you operated in alignment with your own moral code, even when others do not or when they trigger your reactivity? See whether you can connect with this sense of freedom that can arise when you are no longer acting with predictable automaticity but out of true and virtuous choice.

4 Now bring to mind a decision you need to make, sit with it, checking in with the feelings and sensations this gives rise to. If you acted purely in accordance with your own moral compass, how would that feel in your body? What would it look like? What effect would this have on your team, your company, your customers? Let the felt sense of this sink into you, absorbing the effects of this practice.

Summary

Today we explored the nature, extent and the causes of unethical behaviour in the workplace. We established that misconduct is widespread in the corporate world and, to a large extent – but not exclusively – due to the pressure to meet business targets. A review of the scientific literature shed light on deeper causes of unethical behaviour, including subconscious psychological and cognitive biases leading to self-delusion and self-serving judgements, as well as several factors to do with group and organizational cultures.

Subsequently, we explored the role of mindfulness in raising our awareness of any discrepancies between our personal and company values and highlighted the importance of seeing mindfulness as embedded in a larger ethical framework beyond the narrow confines of attention training. We outlined the many different ways in which mindfulness may further socially responsible behaviour and ethical decision-making, most notably through enhanced awareness as a crucial part of several decision-making models and an element often missing in unethical behaviour.

SUNDAY

MONDAY

TUESDAY

WEDNESDAY

THURSDAY

FRIDAY

SATURDAY

To conclude, we introduced a practice to help us reconnect with our virtues from a felt sense in the body rather than as a top-down decision, which will support us in acting with awareness, intentionality and in accordance with our own values.

Fact-check (answers at the back)

1. According to the KPMG Forensic Integrity Survey (2013), the biggest cause of workplace misconduct was due to
a) Lack of awareness of acceptable standards of conduct ❏
b) A lack of communication and training ❏
c) Pressure to meet business targets ❏
d) Selfish motives of self-advancement ❏

2. Unethical actions are often based on self-serving judgements because
a) People are selfish ❏
b) Such judgements require less conscious effort ❏
c) People refuse to consider other perspectives ❏
d) Unbiased opinions will not get them very far in the workplace ❏

3. Mindfulness best supports ethical decision-making when
a) It is practised with the 'right effort' ❏
b) It is narrowly defined as attention training ❏
c) It is seen as a stand-alone tool ❏
d) It is embedded in our value system ❏

4. Evidence suggests that meditation can facilitate socially responsible behaviour by
a) Shifting psychological traits and changing personal values ❏
b) Facilitating cognitive moral reasoning ❏
c) Implementing top-down training ❏
d) Influencing emotional dispositions ❏

5. Which step precedes moral reasoning in Rest's decision-making model?
a) Moral intention ❏
b) Moral action ❏
c) Moral recognition ❏
d) Moral judgement ❏

6. In terms of the links between mindfulness and ethical decision-making which of the following statement is *not* true?
a) Mindful individuals cheat less ❏
b) Mindful individuals value upholding ethical standards ❏
c) Mindful individuals tend to be more principled in their decisions ❏
d) Mindful individuals always act ethically ❏

7. Ethical fading and moral disengagement are ❏
a) Conscious strategies to obscure unethical behaviour ❏
b) Subconscious processes ❏
c) Attributes of unethical people ❏
d) Excuses to justify unethical behaviour ❏

8. The fact that mindfulness encourages openness towards all experiences
a) Can lead to amorality ❏
b) Makes it more difficult to choose the right action ❏
c) Gives us the courage to face up to difficult truths about ourselves ❏
d) Makes ethical decisions easy ❏

9. Metacognitive awareness helps inhibit unethical behaviour by
a) Giving us a choice on how to act due to dissociation from our thoughts ❏
b) Improving the knowledge of our cognitions ❏
c) Connecting us with our morals ❏
d) Making us more aware of the power of our thoughts ❏

10. A focus on inner experience can facilitate ethical behaviour by
a) Making us focus on how good it feels ❏
b) Stressing the importance of the experiencing subject ❏
c) Making us more aware of internal warning signs ❏
d) Helping us concentrate on our emotions ❏

SUNDAY

MONDAY

TUESDAY

WEDNESDAY

THURSDAY

FRIDAY

SATURDAY

SATURDAY

Don't worry, be happy

You may be surprised to find a chapter on happiness in a workplace skills book. We all know that we need to manage stress, be productive, make savvy decisions, perform well and get along with our colleagues. But happiness? Why is happiness important at work? Is that not a luxury that may be nice to have but ultimately not essential in order to hold down a job? However, research has shown that happy people perform better, are more creative and innovative, cope better with stress, have better physical health (so they take fewer days off due to illness!) and are more immune to mental illness. Most managers would agree that this is a compelling business case for encouraging staff to maximize their levels of happiness.

In this chapter we will explore a different understanding of happiness, based on insights into our three in-built causes of suffering, identify when people tend to be at their happiest and explore how mindfulness can help us increase our levels of wellbeing. We will learn some techniques based on these insights to help us practise internalizing happiness in order to hardwire it in the implicit memory of our brain.

What is happiness?

It is safe to say that we all want to be happy. Yet very few people would probably lay claim to this label for any sustainable length of time. By extension, how many people do you know who are happy in their jobs or would rate their job satisfaction a ten out of ten? More likely than not, even if you land your dream job – if there is such a thing – you will most probably end up not being continuously happy either. I would argue that this is due to the fallacy in the very way we tend to define happiness in the first place, namely as a proliferation of pleasant experiences.

First cause of suffering: the brain's negativity bias

For evolutionary reasons, humankind developed a brain that is governed by one overriding principle: to minimize danger and to maximize reward. As we explored earlier in the week, this avoidance of threat and pursuit of rewards has served a powerful purpose in the evolution of humanity: to ensure our survival. While recognizing a genuine threat was a matter of life and death, seeking rewards, while important, was somewhat less critical. If you lived to see another day, you could try your luck again tomorrow to secure your dinner! So over millions of years our brains evolved to be hyper-vigilant with regard to danger and less perceptive of potential rewards. This inherent negativity bias tilted our brains towards detecting possible threats, which are sensed and suspected behind every corner, so to speak, even though today's threats tend to be social ones.

By contrast, positive experiences may seem scarce by comparison and, what is worse, the brain's negativity bias means that you may not even notice them when they do occur (Baumeister et al. 2001). Moreover, unless you make a special effort to dwell on them, they are less likely to leave a trace in your implicit memory, which colours how you feel about your life. So, in order to find happiness, we need to overcome our inherent prioritizing of the negative and shift the focus consciously and deliberately towards the positive. Happiness is so much more elusive than unhappiness!

TIP To see whether this is true for you challenge yourself to make a list of ten good things that happened to you this week and ten things that went wrong. Which events were easier to recall? Which left a stronger imprint on your memory?

Second cause of suffering: grasping

As if this innate imbalance in the way our brain is wired has not made it difficult enough to be happy, human beings compound their own misery by two fundamental and entirely natural, but ultimately dysfunctional and counterproductive, tendencies of the mind, already touched upon on Thursday: desperately to hold on to pleasures and rewards and anxiously to push away any pain, danger or discomfort. Whether it is praise and positive feedback, a lucrative sale, a good working relationship, a successful pitch or a delicious meal, we are rarely content with these isolated incidents and rewards; we quickly expect and even demand more, and when things do not work out we are disappointed.

There is nothing wrong with liking the good things and disliking the unpleasant ones; of course, this is entirely normal. But there is a problem inherent in such likes and dislikes when they turn into clinging or aversion, to use the Buddhist terminology, or greed and fear, to use the jargon of the financial markets. Pleasure and pain, gain and loss, fame and disrepute, praise and blame – they arise and pass and alternate due to circumstances (other people's psychology, events, etc. beyond our control). Attachment to the pleasant side of this equation and the delusion of permanence are doomed to failure and hence breed suffering. Similarly, the misconception that unpleasant experiences will persist makes you vulnerable to depression as you lose the perspective of the changing fortunes inherent in life, not being able to imagine that better days may eventually come. It may sound banal but how often do we get sucked into catastrophizing thoughts, just because one presentation or phone call did not go according to plan, visualizing and anticipating our professional downfall?

Redefining happiness

So, what if the secret to our happiness were this: to be able to enjoy and relish all the pleasant experiences in our life and work without grasping for more, without getting attached to an erroneous expectation of their never-ending proliferation, and, by the same token, the capacity to face up to the unpleasant situations without the inner fight and resistance that create suffering?

If you redefine happiness in this way, as a form of what in Buddhism is called equanimity and non-reactivity, rather than viewing it as the predominance of positive emotions, it is indeed within your grasp to be happy a great deal more, if not most of the time. Why? Because happiness no longer depends on unrealistic conditions that are impossible to fulfil or control in any sustainable way. Pleasant experiences are transient, just like everything else, and making your sense of happiness contingent on them is like building a house of cards. Yet being open to all events and situations, by and large making your peace with whatever arises, is an attitude and habit of the mind that you can learn and achieve when you practise mindfulness. The benefits are life changing and can transform the way you view your job in the process.

TIP *When you no longer react habitually to pleasant and unpleasant experiences you can nourish a sense of equanimity – of no longer wishing for things to be different from what they are. Incline your mind to think 'It's OK as it is.' However, if there are changes to be made to make things better, do not hesitate to initiate them! Notice any resistance to doing this practice and see whether you can consciously let go of it. It does not serve you.*

When are we happiest?

One way to achieve such equanimity is to immerse yourself fully in the present moment with an attitude of openness and curiosity. In other words, not having an agenda in terms of your experience. You need to ensure that you are not just physically going 'through the motions' of whatever you are engaged in; a difficult client call, a boring meeting, a daunting presentation, the dreaded admin tasks that only seem bearable when you engage in pleasant daydreaming, while fantasizing about your upcoming holiday or reminiscing about the big party you went to last weekend – no, to become fully immersed in the present moment means rooting your mind and not just your body in the here and now, rather than time-travelling to a better place, a nicer time...

Third cause of suffering: the wandering mind is an unhappy mind

Recent research has indeed established that people are happiest when their mind does not wander from whatever they are doing at any given time (Killingsworth & Gilbert 2010). Through the use of a mobile application for the iPhone participants from over 80 occupational categories were contacted randomly several times during the day as they went about their life, and asked about their thoughts, feelings and actions. These were recorded on a database in order to establish how often people engaged in mind wandering and to what extent this affected their level of happiness. The results were astounding, establishing that:

1 Mind wandering occurs very frequently and almost half of the time people drifted into this state, confirming that mind wandering indeed seems to be our default state, as established by previous neuroscience research. Interestingly, the pleasantness or otherwise of people's current activity had little bearing on the occurrence of daydreaming.
2 People reported being happier when their mind did *not* wander from what they were currently doing, even when the

activity was not considered particularly enjoyable and even when their mind wandered to pleasant topics.

3 Happiness levels depended disproportionately more on people's *thinking* rather than on their doing – in other words, thoughts were a better predictor of people's happiness levels than the activities they were engaged in.

Our brain's default mode network

So what insights can we gain from this? Mind wandering is indeed our natural, default state, as neuroimaging studies have also established. We have two distinct networks in the brain: a task-positive network that is active when we engage in an activity, and a task-negative, so-called default mode network (DMN), which is active at all other times. In other words, rather than ever being truly 'at rest', our brain's natural baseline is to indulge in mind wandering, from which it departs only when our attention is summoned elsewhere. Whenever we are not specifically working on something, the DMN kicks into action and hijacks our mind with thoughts about the past, the future, other people and ourselves, creating narratives that take us away from experiencing our lives fully and making us unhappy, as, more often than not, the stories we create are made up of worries, concerns, anxiety, regrets, guilt, shame and pending catastrophes.

In other words, rampant mind wandering often is the *cause* of unhappiness, as well as a symptom of it. They say that actions speak louder than words but it seems that the reverse is true! What you think is even more decisive than what you do in terms of your chance of happiness. You may be engaged in a job or activity that you do not find that enjoyable and still have a better chance of being happy if you focus on it entirely than when you indulge yourself in daydreaming about an exotic holiday on a white, sandy beach. In the words of the researchers. According to the researchers, a 'wandering mind is an unhappy mind' as the cognitive feat of self-projection into past or future brings with it an emotional cost.

> *'The present moment is filled with joy and happiness. If you are attentive, you will see it.'*
>
> Thích Nhất Hạnh, Vietnamese Buddhist monk

Try this: staying present

1 Identify a specific task that you do regularly and that leads to feelings of boredom, frustration or resistance of some sort. This may be something like doing the accounts, writing a report, preparing a presentation, creating an Excel sheet, cold-calling, leaving voicemails for clients or any other aspect of your job description that may in some ways dampen your mood or lower your energy.

2 Set an intention to 'stay with' the experience, however unpleasant you find it, and detect your mind's tendency to wander. When it does, as it will inevitably do, note where it has gone and gently bring it back to the present moment. Noticing that your mind has wandered is an indication that you are becoming more mindful and is thus a reason to rejoice rather than beat yourself up!

3 Notice whether there is any sense of aversion to the task in the background of your mind. Without judging yourself in any way, see whether you can gently release this feeling and relax into the experience, noticing its feeling tone without reacting to it.

4 To help your mind focus on the present moment, bring to the experience a sense of curiosity or beginner's mind, as we have already practised. Noticing details about the task will help you enjoy it more as your mind will settle into the present moment.

How mindfulness promotes happiness

How can we expect to be happy when we do not even turn up for our experience as we time-travel to the past or the future and, when we finally do, we refuse to accept the constant flux that is part of the human condition and wish for things to be different from what they are? Having grasped the key sources of human unhappiness and distress it is easy to see how mindfulness might support us in reducing, if not removing, them.

Direct experience versus mental narratives

Living and valuing the present moment and direct experience for their own sakes naturally reduces mind wandering and hence tendencies to get hijacked by the narratives we create in our head through the DMN, featuring rumination on negative thoughts and feelings, as well as worry and anxiety.

Absorbing the positive

By encouraging us to notice, appreciate and absorb the often neglected positive, as well as neutral, aspects of our experience rather than focus solely on the negative, mindfulness can help us redress our brain's in-built negativity bias.

Equanimity

At the same time we learn to notice and hence transcend the slavish pursuit of pleasant experiences and the avoidance of unpleasant ones and instead to open to and be more at peace with the whole gamut of our experience.

Being versus doing

Mindfulness takes us out of 'doing mode', our habitual way of living by which we constantly diagnose what is missing or wrong and strive to fix or improve the current situation. Our obsession with closing the gap between what is and what we would like there to be (discrepancy-based processing) is an integral part of our distress. This tendency, at the heart of our Western culture, is a major driver of our unhappiness. Mindfulness stops us from perceiving our life and work from the perennially dissatisfied perspective of such processing and teaches us that we are complete and whole, just as we are, allowing us to let go of any such striving. Relating to experience mindfully means to reside in the realm of being.

Gratitude

Mindfulness can foster a sense of gratitude, allowing you to appreciate, not just cognitively with your mind, but as a feeling in your heart, all the pleasant and positive things that have been offered to you at and through your work. These may be:

- a kind and supportive attitude by your boss or colleagues
- a decent salary to enable you to live comfortably
- a safe and pleasant working environment
- interesting work
- opportunities to develop yourself
- your own talent, skills and resilience.

Raising the happiness set point

Neuroimaging research has confirmed that mindfulness can indeed raise what has been termed the happiness set point, the biologically determined average level of happiness around which our emotional range converges. According to research dating back to the 1970s, this has been shown to remain relatively stable throughout people's lives, irrespective of their specific experiences, returning to the individual base level a short while after either happy or distressing events have been digested. Apparently, whether you win the lottery or you become paraplegic, within one year you will end up back at your personal set point of happiness! Such individual differences have been confirmed by brain scans that have demonstrated that people with more baseline activation of the left versus the right prefrontal areas tend to be happier than those where the right side of the PFC is more active. Yet it has also been shown that mindfulness can incrementally raise this set point: the more hours of mindfulness practice you have under your belt, the more the activation ratio in your brain tilts towards the left. These results are apparent even after only eight weeks of mindfulness training, as a study by Davidson and Kabat-Zinn at the biotech company Promega (2003) has found: compared to a control group, course participants showed a shift of the happiness ratio towards the left PFC after the training, coupled with a reported reduction in stress and anxiety levels and an increase in energy. Moreover, the study also demonstrated a strengthening of participants' immune system, as evidenced by the amount of flu antibodies in their blood after a flu jab. After only eight weeks, mindfulness had improved both their health and their happiness!

Try this: mindfulness for increasing happiness

To redress the brain's negative bias and increase your experience of happiness, practise absorbing the good things that happen to you in the following way. This is not about chasing positive experiences – as we have seen, this is futile and hence more likely to make you miserable. However, it is about appreciating what is already there and allowing it to increase your happiness set point:

1 **Notice**: make a habit of noticing the good things that happen to you. This could be your colleague, boss or client thanking you for a piece of work you have done or a compliment you receive, something you achieve or complete at work, a gesture of kindness towards you or just the fact that it's a sunny day or that you are having a nutritious meal. Give yourself permission to let this event register as a positive experience in your heart and mind, rather than mentally moving on to the next thing and letting it evaporate straight away. See how this feels.

2 **Attend**: place the spotlight of your attention on this positive experience for half a minute or so, really resting on it and giving your brain a chance to make some new connections (remember: 'Neurons that fire together, wire together')!

3 **Absorb**: Soak up and absorb the positive experience consciously, letting it infiltrate your body and become part of your felt sense of reality at that moment. By repeating this step every time you have even a small positive experience, you will start lifting your felt sense of happiness bit by bit.

TIP *Make this exercise a daily staple. If you want to give happiness a fighting chance, you need to counteract the in-built negativity bias of the brain by an equally, if not more, powerful antidote. Rather than waiting for really life-changing events, of which there are few and far between, use a steady trickle of small, good daily experiences, gradually to fill your brain with a pervasive sense of wellbeing.*

Summary

Today we started off by questioning the conventional understanding of happiness as a proliferation of positive experiences and explored the three causes of human suffering: first, the in-built negativity bias of our brain, which has developed through millions of years of evolution to make us hyper-sensitive to threats and danger; second, our tendency to grasp for pleasant experiences and push away unpleasant ones, which makes us unable to deal with the impermanence of all experiences; and third, the tendency of the human mind to wander away from the present moment, making it challenging for us to live fully in the here and now.

We proposed a definition of happiness as the ability to be at peace with both pleasant and unpleasant experiences without reacting with clinging or aversion. We then explored how mindfulness can help us overcome the three causes of suffering we identified. Mindfulness offers a different, being-based way of relating to experience from our habitual discrepancy-based processing that is aimed at reducing the gulf between 'what is' and what we would ideally like. We shared some tips for practising equanimity and for raising our happiness set point.

Fact-check (answers at the back)

1. The negativity bias in the brain originates in
   a) Our thoughts ❏
   b) Our emotions ❏
   c) Evolution ❏
   d) The brain ❏

2. Negativity bias means that
   a) Negative experiences outweigh positive ones ❏
   b) The brain is more sensitive to negative experiences ❏
   c) We tend to see things negatively ❏
   d) If we expect negative things to happen, they will ❏

3. Which statement is *not* true about the human tendency to cling to the pleasant and push away the unpleasant experiences?
   a) It leads to suffering ❏
   b) It is natural ❏
   c) It is unethical ❏
   d) It compounds the brain's negativity bias ❏

4. Equanimity means
   a) A state of non-reactivity ❏
   b) Being fair in your judgements ❏
   c) Liking everything the same ❏
   d) Being happy ❏

5. Happiness can be defined as
   a) A predominance of pleasant experiences ❏
   b) The absence of negative experiences ❏
   c) A constant state of wellbeing ❏
   d) Being OK with whatever arises ❏

6. Mind wandering occurs
   a) When we are engaged in an activity we do not enjoy ❏
   b) When we are happy ❏
   c) Frequently and for many people ❏
   d) When we are unhappy ❏

7. People tend to be happiest when
   a) They are engaged in pleasant activities ❏
   b) They are thinking pleasant thoughts ❏
   c) Their minds do not wander from what they are doing ❏
   d) Their minds are wandering ❏

8. Which statement is *untrue* about the default node network?
   a) It is a restful and rejuvenating brain state ❏
   b) It is active when we are not engaged in a task ❏
   c) It creates stories about the past or future ❏
   d) It revolves around other people and ourselves ❏

9. What do we mean by the 'doing mode'?
   a) Being proactive ❏
   b) Being busy ❏
   c) The tendency to improve things through constant doing ❏
   d) Being efficient and getting things done ❏

10. Which of the following
    statements is false:
    Discrepancy-based
    processing is

a) The opposite of the
   'being mode'   ❑

b) A synonym for 'doing mode'   ❑

c) Perceiving experience
   from a position of finding
   it lacking   ❑

d) A way of making things
   better   ❑

7 × 7

Seven key ideas

1 **Befriend the present moment:** it is the only one you will ever have.
2 **Practise acceptance:** do not fight 'what is'; it is already here.
3 **Go beyond thinking:** there is an alternative to being lost in thought; it is called awareness.
4 **Keep breathing...** and *know* that you are breathing! The breath is always available to you, to ground you and bring you back to the present moment.
5 **Do not take things personally:** if you look closely enough, most unpleasant things that happen to you do not have your name tag on it!
6 **Be kind to yourself:** beware of self-critical judgements.
7 **Be mindful:** it does not matter what you do or how much you enjoy it, you will feel better if you do it mindfully.

Seven best resources

1 **Best introduction to mindfulness:** Mark Williams and Danny Penman, *Mindfulness: A practical guide to finding peace in a frantic world* (Hachette, 2011). This book contains the complete eight-week MBCT course developed at Oxford University in an easy-to-follow format, with many simple but powerful practices to integrate into your daily life. It also contains a CD with accompanying meditations.
2 **Best free guided meditations:** this page contains all of the meditations from the book *Mindfulness: A practical guide to finding peace in a frantic world* as well as many other resources.
http://franticworld.com/free-meditations-from-mindfulness/

3 **Best introduction to mindfulness at work:** Shamash Alidina and Juliet Adams, *Mindfulness at Work for Dummies* (John Wiley & Sons, 2014). This book is a comprehensive guide to mindfulness at work and covers how to practise mindfulness as well as implement mindfulness training in the workplace, including plenty of invaluable resources.

4 **Best book on mindful leadership:** Janice Marturano, *Finding the Space to Lead: A practical guide to mindful leadership* (Bloomsbury Publishing USA, 2014). Marturana describes the nature and benefits of mindful leadership and shares a variety of simple ways to cultivate it. Many of the meditations are available in audio at www.FindingtheSpacetoLead.com

5 **Best Buddhist wisdom on mindfulness at work:** Thich Nhat Hanh, *Work: How to find joy and meaning in each hour of the day* (Parallax Press, 2013). One of the best-known Buddhist monks adapts Buddhist teachings to the modern workplace, showing how one might apply mindfulness to all aspects of the working day.

6 **Best neuroscience book drawing on Buddhist wisdom:** Rick Hanson, *Buddha's Brain: The practical neuroscience of happiness, love, and wisdom* (New Harbinger Publications, 2009). Hanson, a neuropsychologist and meditation teacher, combines neuroscience with contemplative wisdom to explain how to strengthen your brain for more happiness, love and wisdom.

7 **Best neuroscience-based guided meditations CD set:** Rick Hanson and Richard Mendius, *Meditations to Change Your Brain: Rewire your neural pathways to transform your life* (Sounds True, 2010). This set contains introductions to how mindfulness works on the brain, as well as neuroscience-based guided meditations.

Seven great companies

1 **Google:** the technology company introduced a programme called Search Inside Yourself, led by Chade-Meng Tan, its Jolly Good Fellow, to increase emotional intelligence

using mindfulness, backed by scientific research. The vision behind this programme is to bring mindfulness and peace to the workplace. The programme is now offered to organizations outside the Googleplex.

2 **Aetna:** the health insurer offers its workers meditation classes. Nearly a third of the company's 50,000 employees have taken a class. According to the company, participants show increased productivity and report less stress and pain. More than one-quarter of the company's workforce of 50,000 has participated in at least one class. Participants report a 28-per-cent reduction in their stress levels on average, a 20-per-cent improvement in sleep quality and a 19-per-cent reduction in pain. They also gain an average of 62 minutes per week of productivity each, which Aetna values at $3,000 per employee per year. Demand for the courses continues to rise and all classes are overbooked.

3 **Sounds True:** a multimedia company dedicated to disseminating spiritual wisdom, Sounds True is one of the world's largest publishers of spoken words and spiritual teachings and is one of the world's first organizations to operate with genuinely integral principles, with an emphasis on multiple bottom lines of purpose, people, profit and planet.

4 **Headspace:** founded in 2010, by Andy Puddicumbe, a former Buddhist monk, and Rich Pierson, who has a background in marketing and new brand development. Based on a mission 'to make meditation accessible, relevant and beneficial to as many people as possible', Headspace created a meditation smartphone app, which teaches simple meditation techniques for improving physical and mental wellbeing. Among its clients are firms such as Credit Suisse, KPMG and Deloitte.

5 **Intel:** mindfulness at Intel began when a handful of committed people started meeting regularly in a conference room to practise. The Awake@Intel Program was created in an effort to bring the benefits of mindfulness to the company's workforce. The training promotes stress reduction in a culture where employees 'feel that if they weren't stressed it would mean they're not working hard enough'. So far more than 1,500 employees have completed the nine-week, 90-minutes-per-session Awake@Intel

programme. According to participant feedback, the benefits include 'improved wellbeing, creativity and focus, reduced feelings of stress and stronger engagement in meetings and projects'.

6 **Salesforce:** founded in 1999 by Marc Benioff, this is a cloud computing company headquartered in San Francisco, California. It is renowned for its efforts in philanthropy and social activism and for providing more than just financial benefits to its employees. The Salesforce.com Foundation donates 1 per cent of the company's resources (defined as profit, equity and employee time) to support organizations that are working to 'make the world a better place'.

7 **Apple:** Following the example of their late CEO, Steve Jobs, employees of the tech giant are allowed to take 30 minutes each day to meditate at work, where they can access classes on meditation and yoga, as well as the use of a meditation room.

Seven inspiring people

1 The Tibetan Buddhist spiritual leader the **Dalai Lama** played a central role in bringing together Eastern contemplative wisdom and the emerging field of Western neuroscience when he asked neuroscientist Richard Davidson in 1992 to explore the effects of meditation on the brain. This started a fruitful and ongoing cross-fertilization of these two hitherto separate fields that has led to important advances in the field of neuroplasticity as well as fuelling interest in the practice of mindfulness in the West.

2 **Thich Nhat Hanh** is a Vietnamese Buddhist monk, teacher, author, poet and peace activist. He has published more than a hundred books, including more than 40 in English. He is active in the peace movement, promoting non-violent solutions to conflict and was nominated for the Nobel Peace Prize by Martin Luther King in 1967.

3 **Matthieu Ricard** is a Buddhist monk who has been described as the happiest man on earth, following fMRI brain scans at the Laboratory for Affective Neuroscience

in Wisconsin, which recorded an 'off the charts' state of positive emotions (-0.45 on a range where -0.3 is described as 'beatific'). His advice is: 'Being happy is about raising your "baseline". It's not about seeking sudden fireworks or euphoric experiences. The first step to take is to realize that you want to improve – that the world is not a mail-order catalogue for our fantasies and desires and that we have a relatively limited control over those transient, illusory conditions.'

4 **Jon Kabat-Zinn** is Professor of Medicine Emeritus at the University of Massachusetts Medical School and founder of its Stress Reduction Clinic and the Center for Mindfulness in Medicine, Health Care, and Society. Through his structured eight-week course in Mindfulness-Based Stress Reduction (MBSR) for patients with chronic pain, stress and illness he introduced mindfulness to the West in the 1970s, taking it out of its Buddhist framework and making its teachings widely available. MBSR is now offered by many hospitals, medical centres and health-maintenance organizations.

5 **Eckhart Tolle** is a spiritual teacher and author who, at the age of 29, experienced a deep inner transformation that radically changed the course of his life. He devoted many years to understanding, integrating and deepening that transformation and started working with individuals and small groups as a counsellor and spiritual teacher. Tolle is the author of the number-one *New York Times* bestseller *The Power of Now* (translated into 33 languages) and the highly acclaimed follow-up, *A New Earth*, which are widely regarded as two of the most influential spiritual books of our time.

6 **Arianna Huffington** is the co-founder, chair, president and editor-in-chief of the *Huffington Post*, a nationally syndicated columnist and author of 14 books. She believes that mindfulness is at the heart of everything and has been meditating regularly since the age of 13. She is a sought-after speaker on how mindfulness can be integrated into different aspects of our lives and work, redefining success in her book *Thrive: The third metric to redefining success and creating a life of well-being, wisdom and wonder* (W.H. Allen, 2015).

7 The billionaire and founder of hedge fund Bridgewater Associates **Ray Dalio** has been practising transcendental meditation for over 40 years. He famously declared that 'meditation, more than any other factor, has been the reason for what success I've had.'

8 **Steve Jobs** is best known as the creative genius behind the innovative and groundbreaking products of Apple. Somewhat less known is the fact that he had been a long-term regular meditator who attributed his creativity to his contemplative practice.

Seven great quotes

1 'You can't stop the waves, but you can learn to surf.' – Jon Kabat-Zinn
2 'Don't believe everything you think. Thoughts are just that – thoughts.' – Allan Lokos
3 'Our own worst enemy cannot harm us as much as our unwise thoughts. No one can help us as much as our own compassionate thoughts.' – Buddha
4 Whatever the present moment contains, accept it as if you had chosen it. Always work with it, not against it.' – Eckhart Tolle
5 'Pain is inevitable, but suffering is optional.' – Anonymous
6 'Mindfulness isn't difficult, we just need to remember to do it.' – Sharon Salzberg
7 'Life only unfolds in moments. The healing power of mindfulness lies in living each of those moments as fully as we can, accepting it as it is as we open to what comes next – in the next moment of now.' – Jon Kabat-Zinn

Seven things to do today

1 **Mindful listening:** next time you have a chat with a colleague, a client or your boss, set an intention to give them your full attention, taking in not only their words but also what remains unsaid, their gestures, facial expression,

their intentions. Resist the urge to chip in and share your thoughts. Let them speak without interrupting them. Listen from their agenda, from a perspective of wishing them well rather than judging what they say and whether you agree with them. Being fully present without judgement is a great gift to the people around you.

2 **Mindful speaking:** be intentional and mindful about what you say and how you say it. Consider the effect it may have and whether it will be harmful or beneficial to others, or whether you are just saying it to make yourself feel better by complaining or judging.

3 **Mindful walking:** when you walk to a meeting, to buy lunch or just to the bathroom or the photocopier, do so mindfully. Connecting your breath with the movement, consciously notice the sensations in your feet and legs as you move. Do not rush – rejoice in every step. In the words of Thich Nhat Hanh: 'Walk as if you are kissing the Earth with your feet.'

4 **Mindful eating:** experiment with eating one meal or snack mindfully at work. Be intentional about the choice of food and take your time, savouring the experience, the colour, smell, texture and finally the taste of the food. Resist the temptation to read your emails while you eat. They can wait until afterwards. Chew with awareness and notice the urge to swallow. See how this changes your experience of eating.

5 **Mindful emailing:** next time you send an email, take a couple of minutes longer to contemplate how it will 'land' with the person receiving it rather than focusing on offloading what you want to say. Before you press the 'Send' button, take three mindful breaths to ensure that this is what you want to say and how you want to say it.

6 **Break your routine:** experiment with stepping out of 'automatic pilot', and do a routine task differently. Choose a different route to work or to your desk, sit in a different chair in a meeting, structure your day or even a task differently. See how this gives you a sense of beginner's mind.

7 **Mindful breathing:** during the day, find opportunities to practise mindful breathing, even if it is just one to three breaths at a time. Take an external event as your cue – for example every time you take the lift or elevator or when

you wash your hands or when the phone rings. As Thich Nhat Hanh suggests, you can treat your ringing phone as a mindfulness bell, reminding you to take a mindful breath before you answer it to ensure your full presence in the ensuing conversation.

Seven trends for tomorrow

1 **Mindfulness in organizations:** given that the leading cause of sickness absence tends to be mental ill health, mindfulness is well positioned to become an integral part of standard corporate learning and development initiatives. As Sally Boyle, head of human capital management at Goldman Sachs, put it: 'In years to come we'll be talking about mindfulness as we talk about exercise.'

2 **Compassion training:** compassion training is rising in popularity as a standalone intervention. Although not strictly speaking part of mindfulness, 'lovingkindness', as it is often called, is often practised alongside mindfulness and has a growing body of evidence supporting its salutary effects on psychological wellbeing as well as positive relationships. In this specific practice, people learn to direct the wish that one may not suffer to oneself and then extend the same wish to others, friends and 'enemies' alike, finally to include all living beings. This practice is based on the Buddhist belief that all beings are interconnected in their experience of suffering and their wish to be happy.

3 **Mindfulness in schools:** given encouraging evidence so far, mindfulness may become an integral part of the teaching at schools and other educational establishments. Mindfulness-based interventions may be increasingly employed to help with difficult behaviour as well as conditions such as ADHD.

4 **Mindfulness parenting:** there is growing evidence that introducing both parents and children to mindfulness can be beneficial for family life, particularly for parents in socio-economically disadvantaged families who are also at greater risk of stress. This can lead to less dysfunctional and

destructive behaviour in parents, stress reduction and better behaviour in children.

5 **Mindfulness in health:** although already established in the treatment of depression, mindfulness will continue to be rolled out in the health sector, making it more widely available to people with a long-term physical health condition and a history of recurrent depression. In the UK, latest recommendations include the target of making MBCT for depression available to 15 per cent of people at risk by 2020. To make this possible, 1,200 new MBCT teachers will need to be trained by then.

6 **Mindfulness in the criminal justice system:** following encouraging evidence emerging out of the United States, indicating improved self-regulation, reductions in negative emotional states and reduced drug use, mindfulness may become a standard offering for offender populations, not least to deal with the problem of recurrent depression.

7 **Mindful executive coaching:** as mindfulness is an essential part of being aware and present in the coaching relationship, and an increasing number of executive coaches are espousing a personal mindfulness practice, this field is bound to experience a gradual shift from the still-prevalent goal- and performance-driven approach of executive coaching, to a more mindful and compassionate, being-based approach. Rigorous training is needed to help coaches integrate mindfulness into the very fabric of their coaching presence as well as their communication with their clients.

References

Arnsten, A. F. (1997). Catecholamine regulation of the prefrontal cortex. *Journal of Psychopharmacology*, *11*(2), 151–62.

Arnsten, A. F. (1998). Catecholamine modulation of prefrontal cortical cognitive function. *Trends in Cognitive Sciences*, *2*(11), 436–47.

Arnsten, A. F., and Li, B. M. (2005). Neurobiology of executive functions: catecholamine influences on prefrontal cortical functions. *Biological Psychiatry*, 57(11), 1377–84.

Asch, S. E. (1951). Effects of group pressure upon the modification and distortion of judgments. *Groups, Leadership, and Men.* 222–36.

Bandura, A. (1999). Moral disengagement in the perpetration of inhumanities. *Personality and Social Psychology Review*, *3*(3), 193–209.

Baumeister, R. F., Bratslavsky, E., Finkenauer, C., and Vohs, K. D. (2001). Bad is stronger than good. Review of General Psychology, 5(4), 323.

Brown, K. W., and Ryan, R. M. (2003). The benefits of being present: mindfulness and its role in psychological well-being. *Journal of Personality and Social Psychology*, *84*(4), 822.

Brown, K. W., Ryan, R. M., and Creswell, J. D. (2007). Mindfulness: Theoretical foundations and evidence for its salutary effects. *Psychological Inquiry*, *18*(4), 211–37.

Carlson, D. S., Kacmar, K. M., and Wadsworth, L. L. (2002). The impact of moral intensity dimensions on ethical decision making: Assessing the relevance of orientation. *Journal of Managerial Issues*, 15–30.

Chiesa, A., Serretti, A., and Jakobsen, J. C. (2013). Mindfulness: Top-down or bottom-up emotion regulation strategy? *Clinical Psychology Review*, *33*(1), 82–96.

Chugh, D., Bazerman, M. H., and Banaji, M. R. (2005). Bounded ethicality as a psychological barrier to recognizing conflicts of interest. *Conflicts of Interest: Challenges and solutions in business, law, medicine, and public policy*, 74–95.

Corbetta, M., and Shulman, G. L. (2002). Control of goal-directed and stimulus-driven attention in the brain. *Nature Reviews Neuroscience*, *3*(3), 201–15.

Creswell, J. D., Way, B. M., Eisenberger, N. I., and Lieberman, M. D. (2007). Neural correlates of dispositional mindfulness during affect labeling. *Psychosomatic Medicine*, *69*(6), 560–65.

Dane, E. (2008). Examining experience and its role in dynamic versus static decision-making effectiveness among professionals. In *Academy of Management Proceedings*.

Eisenberger, N. I., Lieberman, M. D., and Williams, K. D. (2003). Does rejection hurt? An fMRI study of social exclusion. *Science*, *302*(5643), 290–92.

Epley, N., and Caruso, E. M. (2004). Egocentric ethics. *Social Justice Research*, *17*(2), 171–87.

Goleman, D. (1996). Emotional Intelligence: why it can matter more than IQ. *Passion, Paradox and Professionalism*, *23*.

Hallowell, E. M. (2005). Overloaded circuits: Why smart people underperform. *Harvard Business Review*, *83*(1), 54–62.

Herndon, F. (2008). Testing mindfulness with perceptual and cognitive factors: External vs. internal encoding, and the cognitive failures questionnaire. *Personality and Individual Differences*, 44(1), 32–41.

Hölzel, B. K., Lazar, S. W., Gard, T., Schuman-Olivier, Z., Vago, D. R., and Ott, U. (2011). How does mindfulness meditation work? Proposing mechanisms of action from a conceptual and neural perspective. *Perspectives on Psychological Science*, *6*(6), 537–59.

Hoyk, R., and Hersey, P. (2010). *The Ethical Executive: Becoming aware of the root causes of unethical behavior: 45 psychological traps that every one of us falls prey to*. Redwood City, CA: Stanford University Press.

Jones, T. M. (1991). Ethical decision making by individuals in organizations: An issue-contingent model. *Academy of Management Review*, *16*(2), 366–95.

Kabat-Zinn, J. (1994). *Where Ever You Go There You Are*. London: Piatkus.

Killingsworth, M. A., and Gilbert, D. T. (2010). A wandering mind is an unhappy mind. *Science*, *330*(6006), 932–32.

Lieberman, M. D., and Eisenberger, N. I. (2008). The pains and pleasures of social life: a social cognitive neuroscience approach. *NeuroLeadership Journal*, 1, 1–9.

Milgram, S. (1963). Behavioral study of obedience. *The Journal of Abnormal and Social Psychology*, *67*(4), 371.

Neisser, U., and Becklen, R. (1975). Selective looking: Attending to visually specified events. *Cognitive Psychology*, *7*(4), 480–94.

Ochsner, K. (2008). Staying cool under pressure: insights from social cognitive neuroscience and their implications for self and society. *NeuroLeadership Journal*, 1.

Pashler, H. J., and Johnston, J. C. (1998). Attentional limitations in dual-task performance. *Attention*, 155–89.

Rest, J. R. (1986). *Moral Development: Advances in research and theory*. Santa Barabara, CA: Praeger.

Rock, D. (2008). SCARF: A brain-based model for collaborating with and influencing others. *NeuroLeadership Journal*, 1(1), 44–52.

Ruedy, N. E., and Schweitzer, M. E. (2010). In the moment: The effect of mindfulness on ethical decision making. *Journal of Business Ethics*, *95*(1), 73–87.

Schneider, S. C., Oppegaard, K., Zollo, M., and Huy, Q. (2005). Socially responsible behaviour: Developing virtue in organisations. *Organisation Studies*.

Shapiro, K. L., Raymond, J. E., and Arnell, K. M. (1994). Attention to visual pattern information produces the attentional blink in rapid serial visual presentation. *Journal of Experimental psychology: Human perception and performance*, *20*(2), 357.

Shapiro, S. L., Carlson, L. E., Astin, J. A., and Freedman, B. (2006). Mechanisms of mindfulness. *Journal of Clinical Psychology*, *62*(3), 373–86.

Smith, E. E., and Kosslyn, S. M. (2013). *Cognitive Psychology: Pearson New International Edition: Mind and Brain*. Pearson.

Teasdale, J. D. (1999). Metacognition, mindfulness and the modification of mood disorders. *Clinical Psychology and Psychotherapy*, *6*(2), 146–55.

Tenbrunsel; A. E., and Messick, D. M. (2004). Ethical fading: The role of self-deception in unethical behavior. *Social Justice Research*, *17*(2), 223–36.

Tencati, A. (2007). Understanding and responding to societal demands on corporate responsibility (RESPONSE): Final Report.

Wager, T. D., and Smith, E. E. (2003). Neuroimaging studies of working memory. *Cognitive, Affective, & Behavioral Neuroscience*, *3*(4), 255–74.

Wolff, S. B. (2005). Emotional competence inventory (ECI) technical manual. The Hay Group. Retrieved 31 January 2010.

Zimbardo, P. G. (1973). On the ethics of intervention in human psychological research: With special reference to the Stanford prison experiment. *Cognition*, *2*(2), 243–56.

Zollo, M., Casanova, L., Crilly, D., Hockerts, K., Neergaard, P., Schneider, S., and Tencati, A. (2007). Understanding and responding to societal demands on corporate responsibility (RESPONSE): Final Report.

Answers

Sunday: 1a; 2c; 3b; 4d; 5b; 6a; 7c; 8c; 9d; 10a

Monday: 1d; 2c; 3a; 4d; 5c; 6a; 7b; 8d; 9a; 10d

Tuesday: 1b; 2d; 3c; 4b&d; 5d; 6c; 7b; 8c; 9d; 10a

Wednesday: 1b; 2d; 3a; 4d; 5b; 6c; 7d; 8b; 9c;10a

Thursday: 1b; 2d; 3b; 4d; 5c; 6a; 7a; 8d; 9c; 10b

Friday: 1c; 2b; 3d; 4a; 5c; 6d; 7b; 8c; 9a; 10c

Saturday: 1c; 2b; 3c; 4a; 5d; 6c; 7c; 8a; 9c; 10d